MY REDEEMER

Christ the Creator

LESLIE M. JOHN

Leslie M. John

MY REDEEMER – CHRIST THE CREATOR

Leslie M. John

MY REDEEMER

Christ the Creator

LESLIE M. JOHN

My messages are simple thoughts generated in me after reading Bible and various books. My main purpose is evangelism, and not offending any individual or organization. Although a small content from my previous book 'My Redeemer' is reproduced in this book, this E-Book is not intended to replace the first edition.

My writings are deposited with Library of Congress Copyright Office, 101 Independence Avenue, SE

Washington, DC 20559-6000, USA, and certificates obtained. All Scriptures in electronic format are from King James Version (KJV) from Open domain and from license obtained.

ISBN-10:0-9890283-5-6
ISBN-13:978-0-9890283-5-6

Leslie M. John

Table of Contents

Leslie M. John

Leslie M. John

INTRODUCTION
PASS THE MESSAGE ON

JESUS CHRIST IS COMING SOON

"He which testifieth these things saith, Surely I come quickly. Amen. Even so, come, Lord Jesus. The grace of our Lord Jesus Christ be with you all. Amen". (Revelation 22:20-21)

O, what a blessed assurance our Lord Jesus Christ gave us that we will see Him face to face when comes again. He is coming again soon! It is not by silver and gold by which we are saved but we are saved by the precious blood of Lord Jesus Christ who gave us salvation free of cost. He saved us from perishing and gave us everlasting life because we believed in Him that He is the Son of God, very God Himself, incarnate in the form of servant in the likeness of man and dwelt among us. It is indeed amazing that such a great God at whose command storms calm down came down and dwelt among us and gave His life for our sake in order to justify us and reconcile us unto Himself.

Lord Jesus Christ revealed His promise to John that he is coming again as written in the book of

7

Revelation. In reply John says, "Even so, come, Lord Jesus." We praise God every day for the hope he bestowed in us that he will receive us, saved by His blood. We are the members of His body, the Church, and He is the head of the Church. When the "Lord Himself shall descend from heaven with a shout, with the voice of the archangel, and with the trump of God: and the dead in Christ shall rise first: Then we which are alive and remain shall be caught up together with them in the clouds, to meet the Lord in the air: and so shall we ever be with the Lord". (Cf. 1 Thessalonians 4:16-17).

We are so glad that we will receive our rewards at the judgment seat of Christ in the mid-air and after a period of seven years we will descend along with our Lord Jesus Christ onto the Mount of Olives at Jerusalem and reign with Him. The blessing that at the end of the thousand years we will not be judged for our sins, but will continue to be with the Lord Jesus Christ and reign for ever and ever is so comforting to us. The wicked and the unjust will be judged and will be cast in to the lake of fire along with Satan and his fallen angels. John ardently desired that Jesus should come soon and the last verse in the Bible bestows on us the grace of Lord Jesus Christ.

Leslie M. John

"The grace of our Lord Jesus Christ be with you all. Amen" (Revelation 22:21)

Lord Jesus Christ said on the "Sermon on the mount" that if any one hears His words and follow them he will be like the one who builds his house upon a rock; the might descend, or the floods might hit the house, or the winds might beat that house, but nothing will happen to the house, because the foundation is upon the rock and, therefore, is strong. On the contrary if anyone does not hear the words of Lord Jesus Christ and does not follow them, his construction of the house will be like the one, who builds it upon the sand. When the rain descends, or when the floods come about, or when the winds blow on to his house it would be blown off.

The faith in Jesus as our Lord and accepting Him as our personal Savior is so comforting that we have everlasting life in glorified bodies. Lord Jesus Christ bore our sins on the cross of Calvary and paid for our sins once and for all. Whoever believes in Him shall not perish but have everlasting life.

Our first parents in the garden of Eden were curious to know as to what happens if they ate fruit

Leslie M. John

from the forbidden tree and such curiosity never ceased even among the present generation who become the date setters for the coming of Jesus in spite of the assertion of Jesus that none but the Father only knows His coming again. Until He comes may we proclaim the Gospel of Jesus Christ instead of finding the probable date of His coming?

This good news has been passing on through His servants to as many as possible from the time the Holy Spirit came upon those who were waiting for him at Jerusalem after the ascension of Lord Jesus Christ. He is in us and wants us to proclaim His Gospel.

The good news of our Lord Jesus Christ proclaimed will not go in vain. It will achieve its purpose for which it was sent. The word of God proclaimed either through the mouth or through the written media will certainly achieve its purpose for which it was sent. We may not see the results immediately but God knows where the fruit lies.

"So shall my word be that goeth forth out of my mouth: it shall not return unto me void, but it shall accomplish that which I please, and it shall prosper in the thing whereto I sent it". (Isaiah 55:11)

Leslie M. John

"And Jesus came and spake unto them, saying, All power is given unto me in heaven and in earth. Go ye therefore, and teach all nations, baptizing them in the name of the Father, and of the Son, and of the Holy Ghost: Teaching them to observe all things whatsoever I have commanded you: and, lo, I am with you alway, even unto the end of the world. Amen" (Matthew 28:18-20)

Leslie M. John

CHAPTER 1
JESUS THE CREATOR

"In the beginning God created the heaven and the earth. And the earth was without form, and void; and darkness was upon the face of the deep. And the Spirit of God moved upon the face of the waters. And God said, Let there be light: and there was light. And God saw the light, that it was good: and God divided the light from the darkness. And God called the light Day, and the darkness he called Night. And the evening and the morning were the first day". (Genesis 1:1-5)

"In the beginning was the Word, and the Word was with God, and the Word was God. The same was in the beginning with God" (John 1:1-2)

From John 1:1-2 we understand that our Lord Jesus Christ is the creator. God is Triune: the Father the Son, and the Holy Spirit. They are co-equal, co-existent but their functions are different, and yet they are all One; and God is One. This is mystery and it is very hard to understand!

"And the Word was made flesh, and dwelt among us, (and we beheld his glory, the glory as of the only begotten of the Father,) full of grace and truth". (John 1:14)

What a great statement it is that the Word became flesh and dwelt among us. The Word became a living being and lived among us. The Word was none other than Lord Jesus Christ and in Him we have redemption through his blood, even the forgiveness of sins.

We have redemption from the bondage of sin in none but Lord Jesus Christ, who is the image of the invisible God. He is the first born of every creature and by Him were all the things created that are in heaven, and in earth visible and invisible, whether they be thrones, or dominions, or principalities, or powers. Lord Jesus Christ is the creator and He created everything for Him. He was before all things and by Him all things consist. He is the head of the Church and He is the beginning and the firstborn from the dead. He is Alpha and Omega. He has the keys of hell and death. (Cf. Colossians 1:14-20 and Revelation 1

"In whom we have redemption through his blood, even the forgiveness of sins: Who is the image of the invisible God, the firstborn of every creature:

13

For by him were all things created, that are in heaven, and that are in earth, visible and invisible, whether they be thrones, or dominions, or principalities, or powers: all things were created by him, and for him: And he is before all things, and by him all things consist. And he is the head of the body, the church: who is the beginning, the firstborn from the dead; that in all things he might have the preeminence. For it pleased the Father that in him should all fulness dwell; And, having made peace through the blood of his cross, by him to reconcile all things unto himself; by him, I say, whether they be things in earth, or things in heaven" (Colossians 1:14-20 and Revelation 22:13)

The writer of Hebrews describes in the book of Hebrews Chapter 1 that the Father has appointed His Son, Lord Jesus Christ, the heir of all things and by whom also He made all the worlds. Jesus was the brightness of the glory of the Father, and express image of His person, upholding all things by the word of His power. It pleased the Father to bruise the Son for our sake in order to redeem us from the bondage of sin. Lord Jesus Christ purged our sins and sat down on the right hand of the Majesty on high. Jesus did not die as martyr, or good man, or innocent man, but He voluntarily became sacrifice on behalf us, paid penalty on behalf us in order to redeem us. (Cf. Hebrews 1:1-10 and John Ch.19)

The blood of Jesus, the Son of God cleanses us from all sin, and the entire hope of redemption that we have, the entire hope of eternity, lies in the fact that Jesus got the job done on the cross. Think of Jesus yielding to the shouts of those men who were witnesses at the cross of Calvary that if He was the Son of God He should come down, save Him and save others. If only Jesus yielded to their shouts and gotten down from the cross before He died, He would not have completed the task he took upon Him to accomplish.

When Jesus said, "It is finished he said, "It is finished" because He had accomplished all that He had to accomplish and it was finished. Nothing more needs to be added to our redemption, or nothing more can be added to our redemption. Jesus finished the task and it ended there. It does not need someone else go after Him to complete any task that might anyone think is left behind; no nothing is left behind, and no one needs to do anything more. The task of creation was in the hands of Jesus and He finished it.

Leslie M. John

The task of redemption was in the hands of Jesus and He finished it. It was at the cross when He is about to die, He said, "It is finished" because nothing more needed to be accomplished for our redemption from sin that He died on the cross and rose from the dead on the third day with incorruptible body. We cannot add our good works to the finished work of salvation by Lord Jesus Christ. It is only by grace through faith in Him that saves us from perishing.

Leslie M. John

CHAPTER 2
JESUS HUMBLED HIMSELF

Lord Jesus was in the form of God and did not think it robbery to be to equal with God, but made himself of no repute, took the form of servant, and became like a man and dwelt among us. He was born of the Virgin Mary, by the works of Holy Spirit, and was laid in a manger. He was raised in a poor family. His earthly parents offered turtle doves as offerings (Luke 2:24), which was a provision made for poor and those, who could not offer bull or goat as sacrifice as per Old Testament Law.

In Colossians 1st Chapter verses 15 to 17, there is a clear description that Jesus the creator. He is the image of the invisible God, the first born of every creature, and by him were all things created; yet we see that he took the form of man for our sake. He testified, in Luke 9:58 how poor he was on this earth.

In the book of Hosea the pathetic condition of Israel is seen. Israel, who had been blessed and to whom were the blessings and covenants given, continually fell from the presence of the Lord. In the sight of the Lord, who asked Hosea to marry a prostitute, Israel was similar to Prostitute, dishonest with her infidelity.

God, who was like husband to them had to see her deviation from the honesty and loyalty, had to chastise them time and again. The Lord goes on to say that they are not his people, and he is not their God. He was like a frustrated husband trying to bring them to the path of salvation, yet they erred time and again. This was the reason, why God had to extend salvation to the Gentiles, thus making Jews and Gentiles one in Christ.

It was not a mystery that the Gentiles should be saved but one mystery was certainly there that God would form Church consisting of Jews and Gentiles, and that Church is above Jews and Gentiles. This purpose was hidden in God until it was revealed to us in Ephesians 2nd Chapter.

The Church is the body of Christ. In this Church are no differences as to who is Jew and who is Gentile, but everyone has similar status. In this Church is seen no more distinction of earthly differences of race, ethnicity, clan, color, and nationality. It is the blood of Jesus that saves a man from being

18

condemned to death and eternal destruction. It is the water that Jesus gives that becomes living water for the sinner. It is the life that Jesus gives to sinner that becomes eternal life.

God in his mercy and love for us quickened us in spirit together with Christ and by grace we are saved. He has given us the privilege to be seated together in heavenly places in Christ Jesus. Faith in him alone saved us and not of any good works in us or by us. If the salvation is by works, then anybody could boast of himself/herself by doing good works that he is worthy to receive salvation by himself, and of his good works. This renders the sacrifice of Jesus of null effect.

The very purpose of Jesus coming into this world was to bear on himself, the sins of the world so that whoever believes in him could be saved. If good works of any man could save him, then Christ need not have come to this world. There is a fundamental error in believing that good works of any man would save him from his sins.

"We are his workmanship, created in Christ Jesus unto good works". This was in the plan of God even before the foundation of the world. The good

19

works of a man will not save him but in Christ Jesus we will do good works as a result of having the fruit of the Holy Spirit. "We were without Christ, and aliens from the commonwealth of Israel; We had no hope of having salvation but in the blood of Jesus Christ we are made one.

All this was took place because Jesus became a sacrifice on our behalf, when he took upon himself, our curse, our sin and shed his precious blood upon the cross of Calvary. The salvation is received by his 'grace' through faith in him that he died and rose for our sake, and by accepting his as 'Lord '. He offered himself on the cross so that we may have riches in him. The earthly riches are not true riches. What if a man earns whole earth his soul? We are saved by his precious blood and not of any of our works. We are not purchased by gold and/or silver, but by the blood of Jesus, who paid it as price for our salvation.

Leslie M. John

CHAPTER 3
JESUS THE PASCHAL LAMB

John testified that Jesus was the Lamb of God. The next day John saw Jesus coming toward him and said, "Look, the Lamb of God, who takes away the sin of the world!" John 1:29

It was a typological forecast of the death of our Lord and Savior Jesus Christ, which was presented in Exodus 12. The Paschal lamb was to be slain on the Passover day. The instructions to celebrate the Passover festival were given in strict elegance, style and accuracy in Exodus Chapter 12. The Lord also told them that if they did not slay the Paschal lamb and apply its blood over the doorposts of their houses, it would be disastrous for them, because if the destroyer-angel, who passes that house sees no blood mark on the side posts and the lintels of any house, he would kill the first born in that family; the first born of not only of that family, but also cattle of that house.

"The blood will be a sign for you on the houses where you are; and when I see the blood, I will pass over you. No destructive plague will touch you when I strike Egypt" Exodus 12:13

The LORD said to Moses and Aaron in Egypt, "This month is to be for you the first month, the first month of your year. Tell the whole community of Israel that on the tenth day of this month each man is to take a lamb for his family, one for each household. If any household is too small for a whole lamb, they must share one with their nearest neighbor, having taken into account the number of people there are.

They were to determine the amount of lamb needed in accordance with what each person will eat. The animals you choose must be year-old males without defect, and you may take them from the sheep or the goats. Take care of them until the fourteenth day of the month, when all the people of the community of Israel must slaughter them at twilight. Then they are to take some of the blood and put it on the sides and tops of the doorframes of the houses where they eat the lambs" Exodus 12:1-7

According to the Lord's commandment, the lamb must be without blemish prepared for the Passover. It should be slain on the fourteenth day

Leslie M. John

and roasted over the fire, along with bitter herbs, and bread made without yeast. Each family must to kill one lamb for the members of its family; nevertheless if the family is small and the meat is more than the family could eat, the meat should be shared by neighbor's family.

The love of Christ is revealed here. Neighbor's family joining the meal signifies the love that Jesus wants you and me to share. On the tenth day of the festival, Jesus entered Jerusalem for the celebration of Passover. It was the preparation of the Passover eating on the night before His crucifixion. Even while it was time for His glorification, He was demonstrating that He was born poor. When He sailed on the water, he did it in a borrowed boat. When He ate the Passover, He did it in the borrowed chamber. When He was dead, He was buried in a borrowed Sepulcher. Now, on the day He was to be glorified He rode a borrowed ass's colt.

It is worthy to note here that Christ, in riding the ass's colt, gave us a shadow of his power over the spirit of man, who is born as the wild ass's colt. "But a witless man can no more become wise than a wild donkey's colt can be born a man" Job 11:12.

Leslie M. John

When they brought the colt to Jesus and threw their cloaks over it, he sat on it. Many people spread their cloaks on the road, while others spread branches they had cut in the fields. Those who went ahead and those who followed shouted, "Hosanna!"

"Blessed is he who comes in the name of the Lord!" "Blessed is the coming kingdom of our father David!"

"Hosanna in the highest!" Mark 11:7-10. The King of kings was glorified on the specified day, which is on the tenth day of the Passover festival. The people shouted, "Hosanna!"

Jesus, being the Jew, ate the Passover exactly on the night before His crucifixion. It was just as Jews did according to the instructions God gave Moses and Aaron. Jesus did not fail even in keeping up the Jewish tradition. It was on tenth day that Jesus, the Lamb of God, was glorified.

The night before He was crucified, Jesus ate the Passover just as Jews ate it on the night before the Passover lamb was slain. "Celebrate the Feast of Unleavened Bread, because it was on this very day that I brought your divisions out of Egypt.

Leslie M. John

Celebrate this day as a lasting ordinance for the generations to come. In the first month you are to eat bread made without yeast, from the evening of the fourteenth day until the evening of the twenty-first day. For seven days no yeast is to be found in your houses. And whoever eats anything with yeast in it must be cut off from the community of Israel, whether he is an alien or native-born. Eat nothing made with yeast. Wherever you live, you must eat unleavened bread."

Exodus 12: 17-20 "Get rid of the old yeast that you may be a new batch without yeast--as you really are. For Christ, our Passover lamb, has been sacrificed" 1 Corinthians 5:7

"Therefore let us keep the Festival, not with the old yeast, the yeast of malice and wickedness, but with bread without yeast, the bread of sincerity and truth" 1Corinthians 5:8

Yes! Jesus Christ was beaten up on the cross of Calvary and was crucified exactly on the fourteenth day of the Pass over festival. The roasting of the Paschal lamb on the fourteenth day denotes the exquisite sufferings of the Lord Jesus, even unto death, the death of the cross. His body as the

25

unleavened bread and blood as the wine is available for us as emblems representing His crucified Christ, who commanded us to do eat and drink His blood until He comes for the second time. In doing so we would proclaim His death.

"For you know that it was not with perishable things such as silver or gold that you were redeemed from the empty way of life handed down to you from your forefathers, 19but with the precious blood of Christ, a lamb without blemish or defect." 1 Peter 18:19

Christ suffered in the end of the world (Heb. 9:26), by the hand of the Jews, the whole multitude of them (Luke. 23:18), and for the good of all his spiritual Israel. (7.) Not a bone of it must be broken (v. 46), which is expressly said to be fulfilled in Christ (John. 19:33, 36), denoting the unbroken strength of the Lord Jesus.

"By faith he kept the Passover and the sprinkling of blood, so that the destroyer of the firstborn would not   touch the firstborn of Israel" Hebrews 11:28

There should be no confusion as to whether Jesus kept the law or not. Jesus came in to this world to keep the law and he kept it. Exodus 12:6-8 And ye shall keep it up until the fourteenth day of the same month: and the whole assembly of the congregation of Israel shall kill it in the evening. And they shall take of the blood, and strike it on the two side posts and on the upper door post of the houses, wherein they shall eat it. And they shall eat the flesh in that night, roast with fire, and unleavened bread; and with bitter herbs they shall eat it. Leviticus 23:5-8 In the fourteenth day of the first month at even is the LORD'S Passover.

And on the fifteenth day of the same month is the feast of unleavened bread unto the LORD: seven days ye must eat unleavened bread. In the first day ye shall have an holy convocation: ye shall do no servile work therein. But ye shall offer an offering made by fire unto the LORD seven days: in the seventh day is an holy convocation: ye shall do no servile work therein.

It was on the 14th of Nisan that Jesus ate the Passover and not on the 15th day of Nisan inasmuch as the lamb was to be killed on the evening of 14th of Nisan, the blood was to be taken and stricken on the same night, on the door posts, flesh roasted and eaten in haste, because God killed the first born of Egypt on the same night to

27

force Pharaoh release the Israelites in bondage. Similarly, Jesus, the Messiah was killed on the same night, which is the 14th of Nisan in order to give rest to all the lambs that surrendered their value to Him and cast the shadow on the true Lamb of God, Lord Jesus Christ.

The Lord's Supper is the New Testament. 1 Corinthians 11:23-26 "For I have received of the Lord that which also I delivered unto you, That the Lord Jesus the same night in which he was betrayed took bread: And when he had given thanks, he brake it, and said, Take, eat: this is my body, which is broken for you: this do in remembrance of me. After the same manner also he took the cup, when he had supped, saying, This cup is the new testament in my blood: this do ye, as oft as ye drink it, in remembrance of me. For as often as ye eat this bread, and drink this cup, ye do shew the Lord's death till he come."

Lord Jesus Christ fulfilled the Law of Moses in eating the Passover meal with his disciples and He is the Passover Lamb that was taken by the Jews on 14th of Nisan and was condemned to death on the same night.

Leslie M. John

"Purge out therefore the old leaven, that ye may be a new lump, as ye are unleavened. For even Christ our Passover is sacrificed for us: Therefore let us keep the feast, not with old leaven, neither with the leaven of malice and wickedness; but with the unleavened bread of sincerity and truth". (1 Corinthians 5:7-8)

In eating the Lord's Supper we remember the Lord's death until He comes. Jesus kept the Passover and was slain as Paschal lamb. His blood is available for cleansing us from all our sins. It is because His blood cleansed our sins the destroyer-angel would have nothing do with us. He has passed over us, and so we do not have to fear. Our sins are washed in the blood, that was not only applied to the side posts and the lintels of our body but it has cleansed us totally. We are safe in the hands of our Almighty Jesus Christ. Thanks to God in the name of His one only Son Jesus Christ.

CHAPTER 4
THE PRAYER OF JESUS

The prayer of Jesus, as we read in John Chapter 17, before he was betrayed for crucifixion has some significant truths. There are three divisions clearly seen in the prayer of Jesus. Firstly, he prayed for himself, secondly he prayed for his disciples, thirdly he prayed not for the world but for those who believe on him through the message of his disciples.

John Chapter 17:1-5 contain Jesus' prayer for himself, John 17:6-10 contain Jesus' prayer for his disciples and John 17:11-26 contain Jesus' prayer for those who believe on Jesus through the message of his disciples.

In the prayer for himself he glorified the Father and said that he has glorified the Father and that he may be glorified likewise. Jesus lifted up his eyes to heaven and said to the Father that hour is come and prayed that the Son may glorify the Father. Jesus says that the Father gave power to the Son over all flesh that the Son may give eternal life to as many as the Father gave to the Son. Jesus prays that those who believe in him may have the life eternal that they might know the Father, who is the only true God, and Jesus Christ whom the Father sent. Jesus had earlier said the Father and the Son are one. "I and my Father are one" (John 10:30) and John 14:6 reads "Jesus saith unto him, I am the way, the truth, and the life: no man cometh unto the Father, but by me". (John 14:6)

Jesus prayed to the Father that he may be glorified in the Father with the glory that the Son had with the Father before the world was. (Cf. John 17:1-5) He continued his prayer and says that he glorified the Father and finished the work that the Father assigned to him.

Later, his disciple Peter explained about the glory that the Son of God, Lord Jesus Christ relinquished and came down to this earth in the form of servant and made in the likeness of men. Lord Jesus Christ was in the form of God, and yet he did not think it robbery to be equal to be with God and made himself of no reputation. "He humbled himself and became obedient unto death, even the death of the cross". Jesus came down to this earth to save sinners.

Leslie M. John

The Father exalted him and gave him the name above every name "that at the name of Jesus every knee should bow, of the things in heaven, and things in earth, and things under the earth". Every tongue will confess him that Jesus Christ is the Lord to the glory of the Father. (Cf. Philippians 2:6-11)

At the trial before Pilate Jesus was asked questions. Pilate asked him if Jesus was the King of the Jews. In answer Jesus asked Pilate if he was asking this question on his own or did somebody asked him to inquire about Jesus. Pilate vehemently asserted that he was not Jew and that the nation of Jesus and the chief priests delivered him to Pilate.

Jesus said that his kingdom is not of this world, but his kingdom is yet to come. Pilate continues his questions and asked Jesus if Jesus was the king of the Jews. Jesus said that Pilate had said so and for this reason he was born and for this reason he came into the world that he should bear witness unto the truth. Jesus said that everyone who is of the truth will hear his voice. When people desired that Barabbas be released in preference to Jesus Pilate released Barabbas and scourged Jesus (Cf. John 18:33-40)

Leslie M. John

"Then Pilate therefore took Jesus, and scourged him". (John 19:1)

Pilate questioned Jesus as to where Jesus was from and Jesus did not give him any answer. Pilate then boasted saying the he had the power to crucify Jesus or to realize him. But then, Jesus said to Pilate that he had no power over Jesus except it was given to him from above. (John 19:9-11) The people cried there that Jesus be crucified

"Then answered all the people, and said, His blood be on us, and on our children". (Matthew 27:25)

Pilate then, delivered Jesus to be crucified.

"Then delivered he him therefore unto them to be crucified. And they took Jesus, and led him away". (John 19:16)

CHAPTER 5
SCARLET ROBE AND REED

"And they stripped him, and put on him a scarlet robe. And when they had platted a crown of thorns, they put it upon his head, and a reed in his right hand: and they bowed the knee before him, and mocked him, saying, Hail, King of the Jews!" (Matthew 27:28, 29)

After following the illegal arrest of Jesus, few incidents took place. When it was morning all the chief priests, elders of the people took counsel against Jesus to crucify him. (Matthew 27:1) There is elaborate description about the incidents that took place before his crucifixion. This meditation is about the mockery Jesus faced on behalf of us at the hands of the people who shouted that Jesus should be crucified.

There are three points that need our meditation. One is that they stripped him and put on him a scarlet robe. Second one is about the crown of thorns that they put upon his head. And, the third one is about a reed that they gave in his right hand and insulted him.

There is reason why God instructed Moses to use colors viz. Blue, Scarlet and Purple for curtains in the Tabernacle. The color Scarlet indicates sin and redemption. We claim the promise of redemption as for Israel as it is written in Isaiah 1:18 where it states "Come now, and let us reason together, saith the LORD: though your sins be as scarlet, they shall be as white as snow; though they be red like crimson, they shall be as wool".

The people's desire was to insult Jesus by stripping him and putting on him a scarlet robe (Matthew 27:28). It was divine desire that he bears our sin upon him in order to redeem us from the sin. He paid the price for our sake and bore insult on behalf of us.

Secondly they put on his head a crown of thorns. In the beginning when God created heavens and earth and herbs, plants, animals everything was good. God saw that it was good. In Genesis 1:26 to 31 there is a description as to how God created man in his own image and gave him the authority over every living creature and he saw that it was good.

There is no mention anywhere that thorns and

35

thistles were made for man. But when man transgressed God's command, God cursed the earth for man's sake and it started bringing forth thorns and thistles from then onward.

Thorns also and thistles shall it bring forth to you; and you shall eat the plants of the field; (Genesis 3:18)

When people put the crown of thorns on the head of Jesus they exhibited their insult toward him but it was divine purpose that He should bear our curse upon his head on the cross in order that we may be redeemed of that curse.

Thirdly they gave a reed in his right hand and bowed the knee before him and insulted him saying "Hail, King of the Jews"

A reed is common name for many aquatic plants, most of them large grasses with hollow stem or a very weak flexible strip of cane. They gave this grass piece in the right hand of Jesus and insulted him saying 'Hail, King of the Jews"

Apostle Paul shows the importance of right hand. Speaking about Lord Jesus Christ who is now seated at the right hand of the Father he writes...

"Which he wrought in Christ, when he raised him from the dead, and set him at his own right hand in the heavenly places" (Ephesians 1:20)

Psalmist wrote about right hand of God whom he trusts as the only help and rock of refuge.

"Even there shall thy hand lead me, and thy right hand shall hold me". (Psalm 139:10)

The writer of Hebrews writes about Lord Jesus Christ in Hebrew 1:3 "Who being the brightness of his glory, and the express image of his person, and upholding all things by the word of his power, when he had by himself purged our sins, sat down on the right hand of the Majesty on high"

He writes in Hebrews 1:8 "But unto the Son he saith, Thy throne, O God, is for ever and ever: a sceptre of righteousness is the sceptre of thy kingdom".

Israelites sang a song after crossing the Red Sea. "Thy right hand, O LORD, is become glorious in power: thy right hand, O LORD, hath dashed in pieces the enemy". (Exodus 15:6)

David gave his mother seat on his right hand (Ref:

Leslie M. John

1 Kings 2:19)

The King of kings, Lord of lords, and the God of gods, Lord Jesus who will be seen sitting on the right hand of power and comes in the clouds of heaven (Matthew 26:54) was seen here bearing a reed in shame in his right hand so that we may not be put to shame. He bore shame for our sake. Let us be always thankful to our savior Jesus for taking upon himself our sin and bearing insult on our behalf. Let us worship him in spirit and truth.

CHAPTER 6
BEHOLD THY SON

One of the seven sayings of Jesus on the cross was:

"Behold thy son"... and he continued saying ... "Behold thy mother"

When Jesus therefore saw his mother, and the disciple standing by, whom he loved, he saith unto his mother, Woman, behold thy son! Then saith he to the disciple, Behold thy mother! And from that hour that disciple took her unto his own home. (John 19:26-27)

Leslie M. John

When Jesus was in human form having relinquished his glory to become one like us He honored his mother. When he was hung on the cross he gave the responsibility, to one of his disciples John, to look after his mother. Likewise Jesus also comforted his mother that his disciple John, whom he loved, would be her son from then onwards. Jesus showed great love towards everybody on this earth. His love included healing, forgiving sins, and bearing our sins upon himself.

Jesus was the Son of God, who had divine nature in himself while on this earth, in addition to having human nature. He replied to his mother, once, that he came into this world to do His Father's business.

The Father's business in him and through him was to glorify the Father's name and accept crucifixion bearing our sins upon him in order to redeem us from the bondage of sin. His Father's business was more important for him, but he did not neglect his responsibilities while he was on this earth. Mary the earthly mother of Jesus and Joseph did not find him after their one day's journey while returning from Jerusalem to their native place Galilee. They had been to Jerusalem to celebrate Passover feast.

They supposed that Jesus, who was then a twelve-year old boy, was in their company but having not found him in their company they returned to Jerusalem and found him sitting in the temple learning in the midst of doctors, hearing and asking them questions. They did not find him until three days past and when they found him they were surprised to see that all who heard him were astonished at his understanding and answers. They were all amazed.

At this time Mary, as a human, and concern for him, asked Jesus why he dealt with them in that way and said she and Joseph were seeking for him with sorrow. (Luke 2:44-48) It is at that time that Jesus replied to her saying, "And he said unto them, How is it that ye sought me? wist ye not that I must be about my Father's business?" (Luke 2:49)

But when he was breathing his last on the cross having taken up on himself our sins, he said to his mother, "Behold thy son" and to his disciple John, whom he loved he said "Behold thy mother" Jesus fulfilled every responsibility that was given to him upon this earth before he died for our sake. He was buried and rose on the third day. Later, he ascended into heaven and seated on the right hand

40

of the Majesty. He promised that all those who have accepted him as their savior will have everlasting life and be with him for ever and ever.

41

CHAPTER 7
MEPHIBOSHETH

Two Kings in contrast in Old Testament were those who very often we speak of. One was King Saul and another King David. King Saul was rejected by God, while King David was accepted by God. King Saul sought after the life of David. Saul's daughter was David's wife, yet Saul was after the life of David. Jonathan was the son of Saul.

Jonathan was not only a close relative of David, but was his good friend. Jonathan's son was Mephibosheth. Mephibosheth was very unfortunate in his life, because when he was just a child of five years, his nurse dropped him off her hands, and he became crippled and lame in his both legs. Jonathan requested David, to have mercy on his family. David was extremely kind to Saul's family even though Saul's sought after his soul very often.

David asked Mephibosheth if there was anyone left in the family of Saul, that he could show mercy. Mephibosheth compared himself to a dead dog and inquired David, why he wanted to show kindness. The word, "Dog" is a repulsive and most detested one used in the Bible.

Mephibosheth compared himself as not only a dog but dead one. We see David's kindness was so great that he not only gave Mephibosheth, his inheritance, but also granted him the privilege to dine with him, on his table, along with him, throughout his life. In Ephesians 2:1-3 we read, "...were dead in trespasses and sins..."

In Ephesians 2:4-5 we read, "But God, who is rich in mercy, because of his great love with which He loved us, even though we were dead in trespasses..." But we have become "...joint heirs with Christ..." (Romans 8:17) In Jesus Christ we see a greater love than this. He offered his own life for our sake and granted us salvation free of cost.

He says, "Behold I stand at the door and knock. If anyone hears My voice and opens the door, I will come in to him and dine with him, and he with Me." (Revelation 3:20).

Lord Jesus Christ also said, "I am the living bread which came down from heaven. If anyone eats this bread, he will live for ever; and the bread that I shall give is My flesh, which I gave for the life of the world."(John 6:51)

Leslie M. John

Mephibosheth received inheritance and a place at the king David's table. Jesus calls us to receive our inheritance and have eternal life. Is there still anyone, who reads this message in need of the favor of Jesus Christ? Salvation is free of cost. Jesus paid the price for our sins. We only need to ask him forgiveness and accept Him as personal savior.

CHAPTER 8
HIS PRECIOUS BLOOD

But with the precious blood of Christ, as of a lamb without blemish and without spot: (1 Peter 1:19)

Jesus shed his blood on the cross for our sake that we may have everlasting life provided we believe in him. His blood shed was precious, without blemish and without any spot.

"But he was wounded for our transgressions; he was bruised for our iniquities: the chastisement of our peace was upon him; and with his stripes we are healed". (Isaiah 53:5)

The LORD spoke to Moses and to all the children of Israel that they shall not offer any living thing which was bruised, or crushed or broken, or cut or with any blemish. Any offering that had blemish was not acceptable to Him. (Exodus 12:5, Leviticus 22:17-33)

As was the blood of Jesus precious so was He Himself to the Father and to those who believe in him. Jesus was the living stone, who was rejected

Leslie M. John

by men, but chosen of God.

Speaking at the Lord's Supper Jesus Christ says about remembering his death. He then says to his disciples about eating his flesh and drinking his blood. The institution of the Lord's Supper is applicable to us also. Lord Jesus says that unless we eat the emblems that represent his flesh and drink from the cup that represents his blood we have no life. We were once far off but are brought near to his presence by the blood of Christ.

We are able to enter in his most holy place by the blood of Christ. He is the mediator of the new covenant and to the blood of sprinkling that speaks of better things than that of Abel. The Father gave us peace through the death of our Lord Jesus Christ. Jesus was our shepherd and leads us every day. His death and blood that was shed enabled us to be shepherded by him who is our great shepherd. Jesus Christ's everlasting covenant was the cause for our reconciliation with the Father.

Our fellowship with one another is sustained when we walk in the light just as he was in the light. The blood of Jesus Christ cleanses us from all our sins. He washed us from our sins in his own blood. (Ref.

John 6:53, Ephesians 2:13, Hebrews 10:19, Hebrews 12:24, Hebrews 13:20, 1 John 1:7, Revelation 1:5)

If you believe that Jesus Christ died for you, rose from the dead on the third day and later ascended into heaven your sins God will forgive your sins.

"Come now, and let us reason together, saith the LORD: though your sins be as scarlet, they shall be as white as snow; though they be red like crimson, they shall be as wool" (Isaiah 1:18)

"To whom coming, as unto a living stone, disallowed indeed of men, but chosen of God, and precious" (1 Peter 2:4 – (Cf. Ps 118:22; Isaiah 28:16; 53:5))

Psalmist prophesied about Jesus, that he was rejected but then he became the head stone of the corner (Ref. Psalms 118:22)

Peter wrote "Wherefore also it is contained in the scripture, Behold, I lay in Sion a chief corner stone, elect, precious: and he that believeth on him shall not be confounded". (1 Peter 2:6).

This was prophesied in Isaiah 28:16 and it is as

47

follows:

"Therefore thus saith the Lord GOD, Behold, I lay in Zion for a foundation a stone, a tried stone, a precious corner stone, a sure foundation: he that believeth shall not make haste"

Solomon's temple was the perfect Temple in Jerusalem and it is the true picture of the spiritual temple. The foundation of the Church was laid on Jesus and he is the chief corner stone of the spiritual temple.

For believers in Lord Jesus Christ he is precious but unto those who were disobedient and rejected him he became the corner stone on which the spiritual temple stands. On whomsoever this stone shall fall; it will grind him to powder and whosoever shall fall on this stone shall be broken. (Matthew 21:44)

Two references where Jesus was called the corner stone are: Matthew 21:42, and Acts 4:11-12. Jesus pointed to his own position questioning Jews if they have not read in prophesies that he was the stone which the builders rejected but became the corner stone.

Peter spoke of Lord Jesus Christ and said that the

48

salvation is in Jesus alone and none else. Jesus, who was the stone which Jews rejected he became the corner stone to hold the spiritual temple in its position. (Acts 4:11-12)

"Unto you therefore which believe he is precious: but unto them which be disobedient, the stone which the builders disallowed, the same is made the head of the corner" (1 Peter 2:7)

For those who reject Lord Jesus Christ as savior he is a stone of stumbling, a rock of offence, and they will get hurt, but we are redeemed with precious blood of Lord Jesus Christ and not by corruptible things such as silver and gold and, therefore, we are as lively stones are built up spiritual house, an holy priesthood to offer spiritual sacrifices, acceptable to God by Jesus Christ.

"And a stone of stumbling, and a rock of offence, even to them which stumble at the word, being disobedient: whereunto also they were appointed". (1 Peter 2:8)

"Forasmuch as ye know that ye were not redeemed with corruptible things, as silver and gold, from your vain conversation received by tradition from your fathers" (1 Peter 1:18)

Leslie M. John

"Ye also, as lively stones, are built up a spiritual house, an holy priesthood, to offer up spiritual sacrifices, acceptable to God by Jesus Christ". (1 Peter 2:5

Believing in Jesus will entail us not only to be partakers of his promises but also to be partakers of divine nature. The promises from God are exceedingly precious and they are infallible assurances to us. The promises that God made are in his power to grant to us, and he grants them to us as he pleases. (2 Peter 1:4)

"For it became him, for whom are all things, and by whom are all things, in bringing many sons unto glory, to make the captain of their salvation perfect through sufferings". (Hebrews 2:10)

Leslie M. John

CHAPTER 9
DARKNESS AND LIGHT

"Now from the sixth hour there was darkness over all the land unto the ninth hour." Matt. 27:45

Darkness prevailed on the face of the earth, in the midst of the day light. It was not an eclipse, for it was during Passover that this darkness came upon the face of the earth; nor was it the usual darkness that comes at sunset. It was indeed unusual. During day light hours, a severe darkness brought about by God the father from heaven upon this earth, and more of that on Jesus Christ, His one and only son.

"Woe unto them that call evil good, and good evil; that put darkness for light, and light for darkness; that put bitter for sweet, and sweet for bitter!" (Isaiah 5:20)

This verse is intended as warning to everyone, in all ages. It is to warn of the sins, which are destructive to everyone and to communities as well, exposing every one God's wrath and His holy and righteous

Leslie M. John

judgments. The righteous Lord will cut in sunder the cords of the wicked. And in that day they shall roar against them like the roaring of the sea: and if one look unto the land, behold darkness and sorrow, and the light is darkened in the heavens thereof Isaiah 5:30

Darkness signifies judgment. And it came between the camp of the Egyptians and the camp of Israel; and it was a cloud and darkness to them, but it gave light by night to these: so that the one came not near the other all the night (Cf. Exodus 14:20)

Darkness was one of the plagues of Egypt. Darkness accompanied with fear, sin, and Judgment. It is opposed to luster and honor. Darkness is opposed to wisdom; it is associated with confusion, folly, vexation of Spirit, and calamities. An angel shone light towards Israelites and darkness to Pharaoh and his army when Israelites were just about to cross Red Sea. It was the judgment that Pharaoh and him army were about to face while the children of God were about to cross the great river.

"The sun and the moon shall be darkened, and the stars shall withdraw their shining" (Joel 3:15)

Leslie M. John

Constellation and the sun will be darkened at the second coming of Jesus Christ. Jesus Christ is the light of the world. He is the exact representation of God the father Himself. He was there before the creation of this world, and He will be there at the end of this world also. There was none like Him before and there will none like Him in future.

"And about the ninth hour Jesus cried with a loud voice, saying, Eli, Eli, lama sabachthani? that is to say, My God, my God, why hast thou forsaken me?" (Matthew 27:46)

It is a direct quote from Psalm 22:1. Many years ago David prophesied the death of Jesus Christ. God, the Father saw Jesus, His one and only son, with the sin of the world on his shoulders, and suffering to redeem them. The Holy one of Israel could not bear His Son full with the sin of the world. It was at that time that God the father brought about severest darkness on the face of the earth; it was at that time, Jesus was passing through the darkness; the judgment.

The judgment you and I had to face was on Him. God the father, the Holy God could not see the sin, so He had to leave His son's hand. It is at this time

53

that Jesus Christ cries out, "My God, my God, why hast thou forsaken me?"

It is at this time the Father became God for Him. It is at this time, that the Son of God was separated from the Father. Oh! It is that time that Jesus lost the love of His father, just because He loved you and me. God the father had to turn away His face from His son. Oh! It was then, that the darkness, which no one ever saw before came upon Jesus.

Jesus became criminal before God the father. Jesus became the greatest sinner on the face of the earth, bearing your sins and mine. God punished the sin, and Jesus bearing the sin. The blood of Jesus Christ was shed on the cross, so that your sins and mine could be cleansed in it.

"Ye are all the children of light, and the children of the day: we are not of the night, nor of darkness" (1 Thessalonians 5:5)

It appears pathetic when redeemer of the world was being dragged on the road, with a cross on his shoulder, to Golgotha, but then if it did not happen, what would have been our destiny? It was a cold day with chill weather around, and the Savior of the world, took upon Himself your sins

Leslie M. John

and my sins, and was hung on the cross of Calvary.

Beside Him were two criminals hung on either side. The redeemer of the world, the Savior of the world, became a criminal for your sake and my sake. As if that was not enough a crown of thorns was platted on his head, people spat on His face and even stabbed Him. Large nails were run through his palms and feet on to the cross and huge amount of blood was shed. The blood, the life line of a person was shed so as to cleanse your sins and mine.

Jesus was mocked as King of kings; indeed He was King of kings, but the way they treated Him was unbearable. Who was this person? Yes! He is none other than Jesus, yes! Jesus Christ, the Son of God. Jesus, who is the second person in Trinity, became human for your sake and mine and came into this world to die for our sake, so that we may receive salvation. He did not lie just there in the grave yard like a dead man. He was triumphant over death and rose from the dead, and ascended in to heaven. He is living God. So, now we say boldly,

"And have no fellowship with the unfruitful works of darkness, but rather reprove them" (Ephesians 5:11)

55

Salvation is available free of cost, for all those who accept Him as savior, confessing his/her sins to Him.

"And the fifth angel poured out his vial upon the seat of the beast; and his kingdom was full of darkness; and they gnawed their tongues for pain" (Revelation 16:10)

When the fifth angel poured out his vial, as seen in vision, by John, the whole kingdom of the Antichrist was full of darkness and distress. The city which was the seat applauded policies, the source of all their learning, and all their knowledge, and all their pomp and pleasure, now becomes a source of darkness, and pain, and anguish. Be Saved:

CHAPTER 10
HE IS RISEN

"And when the sabbath was past, Mary Magdalene, and Mary the mother of James, and Salome, had bought sweet spices, that they might come and anoint him. And very early in the morning the first day of the week, they came unto the sepulcher at the rising of the sun. And they said among themselves, Who shall roll us away the stone from the door of the sepulcher? And when they looked, they saw that the stone was rolled away: for it was very great". (Mark 16:1-4)

On the day when Jesus was tried before Pontius Pilate the governor, there was option for people to have either Jesus released or Barabbas released. It was feast day and according to their custom a prisoner of their choice could be released. Pilate asked the people as to whom they prefer to be released; whether it was Barabbas or Jesus. The people cried that Barabbas, a notable criminal be released in preference to that of innocent Jesus. (Matthew 27:15-18)

Pilate knew that Jesus was innocent and that is

57

why he asked the people as to what evil Jesus had committed. A great politician as he was, Pontius Pilate did not want to offend Herod on one side and the people on the other. But the people cried more that Jesus should be crucified. "And the governor said, why, what evil has he done? But they cried out the more, saying, Let him be crucified. (Matthew 27:23) Then Pilate washed his hands and justified himself saying: "I am innocent of the blood of this just person: see you to it". (Matthew 27:24) Pilate acknowledged that Jesus was just person, yet he has handed over Jesus to the choice of people. Thus Pilate is guilty of not showing the justice.

After the Sabbath was past early in the morning Mary Magdalene, and Mary the mother of James went to the tomb where Jesus was laid. A rich man of Arimathaea, named Joseph, who also himself was Jesus' disciple begged for the body of Jesus and he laid it in his own new tomb.

. And laid it in his own new tomb, which he had hewn out in the rock: and he rolled a great stone to the door of the sepulchre, and departed. (Matthew 27:60)

On the tomb, where the dead body of Jesus was laid, a great stone was rolled over it. The tomb was closed with that great stone and it was sealed so that no one could remove the body of Jesus or steal the body of Jesus. All the accusers took care that the dead body of Jesus was not removed from the tomb. The tomb was guarded so that no one could remove or steal the body of Jesus.

"Pilate said unto them, You have guards: go your way, make it as sure as you can. So they went, and made the sepulcher sure, sealing the stone, and setting a guard". (Matthew 27:65-66)

But then, as per the prophecy and as Jesus told beforehand, he rose from the dead and went to Galilee before Mary Magdalene and Mary the mother of James reached the tomb.

Jesus had told that he will rise on the third day, and yet these two missed the timing very badly. Not only this, but before they reached the tomb, they had a big question in their minds as to who will role away the stone?

However they found answer to their question when the Angel of the Lord announced that he was raised from the dead.

Leslie M. John

And, behold, there was a great earthquake: for the angel of the Lord descended from heaven, and came and rolled back the stone from the door, and sat upon it. (Matthew 28:2)

And the angel answered and said unto the women, Fear not: for I know that you seek Jesus, who was crucified. He is not here: for he is risen, as he said. Come, see the place where the Lord lay. (Matthew 28:5-6)

The sacrifice offered up by Abraham was complete when he had laid Isaac, his own only begotten son, on the wood upon the altar by faith that he would be raised by God. Earlier, Abraham had asked his young men, to abide there with the ass, until he went yonder, and return to them after worshipping God. Isaac was Abraham's only begotten son, inasmuch as, he was the promised seed, and Ishmael was a son to Abraham born of his fleshly desire, when he was known as Abram before, and his wife Sarah, who was Sarai, by name, brought Hagar unto him.

This act of Abraham laying down his only begotten son, Isaac, a 'type' of Jesus Christ, was confirmed in Hebrew 11:19. This shows that God is able to raise us up from the dead just as He was able to raise Isaac from the altar, and Jesus from the dead.

Job prophesied about resurrection when he said that his redeemer lives, and that he 'shall stand at the latter day upon earth'. His faith was so great when he said that even though his skin was destroyed by worms, yet he would see God in his flesh. (Job 19:25-27)
Isaiah's prophesy (in Isaiah 26:19) reveals to us that he had confidence that he would be raised from the dead.

We, who are born-again, have great privilege of seeing our Savior face to face. Apostle Paul writes in 1 Corinthians 15:50-53 'that flesh and blood cannot inherit the kingdom of God; neither doth corruption inherit incorruption'. The dead shall rise with incorruptible body. And, when Jesus comes again, not all shall die, but those living shall be 'caught up', and we shall be changed in a moment. "In a moment, in the twinkling of an eye, at the last trump: for the trumpet shall sound".

Paul and Timothy give us great hope (Philippians 3:20-21) that our vile bodies will changed unto glorious bodies.

Leslie M. John

Pillars are the strength of monuments and on the pillars are seen inscriptions or designs that either brings to us some remembrance of those, who responsibly raised them, or help us, admire their beauty. Heaven does not need any pillar to support it, but the New Jerusalem that John saw in his vision coming down from heaven was like a bride adorned for her bridegroom.

In this New Jerusalem were seen the pillars on which were written the names of those, who served the living God, and the names of who those, who they served and represented. Some in the Church at Philadelphia (Rev 3:3-5) had not defiled their garments and they were worthy to receive blessings. God promised that he who overcomes shall walk with Him. Those that overcome stand for the living God, and they are like pillars in the temple of God, and on them are written the names, such as 'name of my God', 'name of the city of my God', which is 'new Jerusalem', and His new name. (Rev 21:2-5)

Lord Jesus was there before the creation and He is the creator. He said "...I am Alpha and Omega, the first and the last..." Revelation 1:11

Leslie M. John

He also said "I am he that liveth, and was dead, and behold, I am alive for evermore, Amen, and have the keys of Hell and of death. (Revelation 1:18)

CHAPTER 11
PASSOVER

Passover is the remembrance of the deliverance of the children of Israel from the bondage of slavery in Egypt. Passover is celebrated for seven days in Israel. It is about remembrance of the killing of the lamb on 14th Nissan and applying its blood on the lintels and door posts of the houses of children of Israel by the children of Israel.

This was to show that the children of Israel were redeemed from the slaughter of their firstborn. God brought this plague in the land of Egypt when Pharaoh refused to let go the children of Israel from out of Egypt as demanded by God through Moses. The first born of every living creature in Egypt was to be killed. That extended from the firstborn of Pharaoh, who was on the throne even unto the captive in the dungeon and the firstborn of cattle. However, the children of Israel were saved from that plague.

It is about the blood of the lamb that saved the children of Israel from that plague. The killing of the firstborn was on the midnight of the first

Leslie M. John

month 'Abib'. The month of Abib' was later renamed as 'Nissan'. (Cf. Exodus Chapter 12)

The LORD gave very firm instructions to the children of Israel that they should tell their children about the Passover and about the mighty power of God that redeemed from the bondage of slavery under Pharaoh. The LORD would, indeed like to hear about Passover from every child of God.

Notwithstanding any writing done by anyone in the past and any details of Passover were elaborated, the LORD would love to see that every child of God remembers about the Passover and tell or write about it. Our God cannot tolerate any child of God worship any other god, other than Him alone. He has neither given His glory to anyone before nor would He allow anyone to take His glory at any time. To honor his pleasure, I as a child of God, saved by Him, washed in the blood of His One and only Son, Lord Jesus Christ, I make this attempt to present the details of Passover.

Exodus Chapter 12 deals with important subject in every Christian's life. In order to understand fully the words "this do in remembrance of me" (Luke 22:19) spoken by Lord Jesus Christ it is imperative that we should know what the LORD said to Moses and Aaron about Passover. The LORD spoke to Moses and Aaron and said to them to that they should convey HIS words to them.

The Chapter commences with the LORD speaking to his beloved servant Moses, who was chosen to lead the children of Israel from out of the bondage of slavery into Canaan, a land described by God himself as the land 'flowing with milk and honey' (Exodus 3:8) The children of Israel suffered under Pharaoh, who made them to be slaves under him and work hard, whereby their lives were made bitter. Pharaoh forced them to make bricks and to do all manner of service in the field with rigor (Exodus 1:14)

The LORD saw the misery of the children of Israel and heard their cry. He sent Moses and Aaron to make a demand that Pharaoh should let them go yonder three days journey from the land of Egypt into wilderness to worship God. Pharaoh refused to let them go on nine occasions when God brought upon the land of Egypt the plagues.

When God brought on them the tenth plague Pharaoh had indeed demanded that the children of

Israel should leave Egypt as soon as possible and the Egyptians were ready to part with their possessions and wealth to any extent to see that the children of Israel leave the land of Egypt as soon as possible. It was after facing the tenth plague that Pharaoh released the children of Israel from the bondage of slavery.

The tenth plague that the LORD brought on them killed the first-born of every Egyptian including that of Pharaoh. The tenth plague was so severe that in order to redeem the children of Israel, the LORD told them through Moses and Aaron that they have to obey Him in keeping the Passover meticulously to every detail in perfection. The LORD said that when the children of Israel do exactly as He demanded of them their firstborn would be spared from the wrath of the LORD, as he passes over their homes.

The LORD spoke to Moses and Aaron and said that, that will be the beginning of the months and it will be the first month of the year to them. The month was known as 'Abib', which in later years was renamed as "Nissan". The LORD said to them that the children of Israel should take a lamb on the tenth day of the said month, either from goat or sheep, which should be blameless. The LORD's instructions continue, thereafter.

A lamb for every household, according to the house of their fathers was to be taken, and if the household was too small for the lamb, the man of the household may share the lamb with his neighbor, next to his house. The number of persons from the neighbor may be counted by him to see that the portion in excess of what was required in that house can be shared by the neighbors. The lamb thus set apart was not a mere lamb but it was their special lamb, which was to be slain on the fourteenth day of the first month of the first year.

The lamb that was to be thus set apart should be their lamb to become part of their family, as if a member of their family, and the children would play with it, until the fourteenth day of the month. The LORD said that the whole assembly of the congregation of Israel should kill it in the evening of the fourteenth day of the first month of the first year. The household was required, then, to take the blood of the lamb and strike it on the two side posts and on the upper door post of the houses, where they were supposed to eat it.

Leslie M. John

They were asked to eat the Passover meal in a very specific way. They were not to violate any instructions from the LORD. Those were special and very important instructions. The flesh of the lamb thus set apart for Passover sacrifice was to be roasted with fire, and eaten with unleavened bread in the night with bitter herbs. (The bitter herbs show their hard labor under Pharaoh and their slavery). The flesh was not be eaten raw, boiled, or soaked in water or moisture. . The head of the lamb, the liver, heart, and lungs should have been roasted and eaten. They were to make sure that there would be no remains of the flesh of the lamb sacrificed.

If by any reason there remains a portion of the lamb until next day it should be burnt with fire. The LORD was particular about their eating in haste. The LORD said to them that while they eat the flesh of the lamb they should have their loins girded, their shoes on their feet, and their staff in their hand, and their eating as to be in haste. It is the LORD's Supper and none of the instructions given to the children of Israel were allowed to be violated. (Their eating in haste shows that they were to leave the land of Egypt immediately after eating).

Leslie M. John

The LORD said unto the children of Israel that He will pass through the land of Egypt that night and smite every firstborn in the land of Egypt, both of man and beast. The LORD said He will execute judgment against the gods of Egypt because He is the LORD.

Pharaoh and his gods took pleasure in the servitude of the children of Israel, whom the LORD loved so much. The LORD had promised the Israel that He shall deliver them from out of the bondage of slavery. The LORD showed His power by humiliating their frog-gods, lice-gods, and all kinds of gods, whom they worshipped.

God gave them plenty of frogs because they loved to worship frogs. This was the tenth plague that God was going to bring upon the Egyptians. In order that the children of Israel may escape this harsh judgment upon them, they were required to have the blood of the lamb on their door posts. The LORD said He shall passes over that home where he finds the blood of the lamb on the door posts and that the plague shall not be upon the household.

This harsh punishment that was brought upon the

Leslie M. John

Egyptians, Pharaoh, and his household, and the sparing of the children of Israel on the day of the Passover shall be a memorial for them, He said.

It was this memorial that was to be kept by the children of Israel. They were required to tell and retell their children about the grace of God that was shown to them. It was a feast for them, and their posterity was required to keep that feast. The feast was holy and they were required to eat unleavened bread for seven days.

The LORD told them that they should put away leaven even on the first day until the seventh day out of their houses in order that they may not be cut off. The first day was holy convocation. The seventh day was holy convocation for them and they were required to take rest and no manner of work was to be done by them. They were only to eat and take rest on that day. They were to observe the feast of unleavened bread on the same day, because it was on that day that the LORD brought them out of the land of Egypt.

Therefore, the observance of Passover feast became an ordinance for them for ever.

It was the fourteenth day of the month of the

Leslie M. John

appointed month and year that the Passover lamb was killed and they were asked to keep the feast until the evening of twentieth day of the month. Whether a man among them was a stranger or born in that land, he shall not have leaven in his house for seven days. Moses told the children of Israel all that the LORD told him and Aaron.

Moses gave them the special directions that they should take bunch of hyssop, and it should be dipped in the blood of the lamb and then strike the lintel and two side posts with the blood that is in the basin. He said to them that none of the children of Israel should go out from their homes until the LORD passes over and until the morning. The blood struck on the lintels and the door posts will serve as identification that the house belongs to one of the children of Israel, who will be spared from the wrath of the LORD.

The children of Israel did as the LORD spoke to them through Moses and Aaron. It was an everlasting ordinance given to them that they and their sons should keep the Passover for ever. Moses told them that they shall keep the Passover even in the land that the LORD that He would give them as He had promised. When their children

Leslie M. John

inquire of them as to what this Passover meant, they were required to tell them that it was the sacrifice of the LORD's Passover, who passed over their houses in Egypt when He killed the first born of the Egyptians and delivered them from the bondage of slavery.

In the midnight of the fourteenth day of the appointed month, the LORD smote every first born in the land of Egypt from the first born of Pharaoh, who was on the throne even unto the captive in the dungeon and the firstborn of cattle. But every firstborn of the children of Israel, who had the blood of the lamb on the lintels and on the side posts of their homes, was spared. The shaken Pharaoh was moved greatly in his heart and yielded to the demand of the LORD through Moses and Aaron.

Pharaoh in his frenzy rose up in the night to see that every first born of the every Egyptian was killed. He rushed to see if his son was safe, but alas! Pharaoh's firstborn was also killed. He hurriedly called for Moses and Aaron by the night and asked them to leave Egypt as quickly as possible and asked them to go and worship their LORD, just as they demanded earlier. Pharaoh also told them that they should take their flocks and herds and be gone and requested to bless him. Egyptians were urgent upon the children of Israel that they should hastily leave Egypt fearing that they all would, otherwise, be dead.

The children of Israel took their dough before it was leavened, their kneading troughs and left the place. Before they left they borrowed the jewels, silver, gold and raiment from the Egyptians. The LORD showed favor to them that the Egyptians gladly gave all that they needed. The children of Israel took all that they can from the Egyptians and left for Succoth from Rameses.

The men of Israel were about six hundred thousand on foot besides women and children. They all went with their flocks, herds, and cattle. The food that they had was of unleavened cakes made out of dough, which they brought forth from Egypt. The dough was not leavened. They were indeed driven out of Egypt because of the lament and cry that came upon Egypt by the slaughter of their firstborn by the LORD. They witnessed in their homes their firstborn was killed by the LORD. As they hurriedly left Egypt they did not bring from Egypt any other kind of food, and, therefore, they made use of the dough to make cakes of unleavened bread.

The LORD helped them to have unleavened bread. Their exodus was so fast and urgently forced upon them that they could not tarry even for a little while there after the firstborn of the Egyptians were killed by the LORD.

It was on the same night that when the exodus of the children of Israel took place from the land of Egypt that the entire host of the LORD also went out from the land of Egypt. It was the evening when their Passover lamb was killed; and the midnight at which the LORD executed judgment on Egyptians was very important in the lives of the children of Israel. It was the night when the firstborn of all the Egyptians were slaughtered and it was to be much observed unto the LORD by the children of Israel for delivering from their slavery. They are, indeed, to remember their past lives, when they served their masters in Egypt and made bricks for them and did all manner of hard labor.

It was the night when they are, indeed, to remember how God gave them plenty of Jewels, gold and silver of Egyptians when they were leaving Egypt. They were harassed many years and not

75

paid their due wages; and the LORD paid them when Egyptians forced them to leave with plenty of affluence because they could not tolerate the agony they suffered under the Almighty God.

The vengeance belongs to the LORD, and rightly so, the Egyptians were punished by Him for harassing the children of Israel, the people, whom God loved very much. This Passover needs to be remembered by the generation of the Children of Israel for ever and ever. It was an everlasting ordinance.

CHAPTER 12
THE LORD'S SUPPER

There are four clear references (Matthew 26:26, Mark 14:22, Luke 22:19 and 1 Corinthians 11:24) where Lord Jesus Christ said, 'take eat; this is my body'. Likewise there are four clear references where Lord Jesus Christ said, 'my blood'.

Matthew, Mark and John, and Apostle Paul wrote that when Lord Jesus broke the bread he said 'take, eat; this is my body'. Luke, the historian, who touched the different themes of the subject did not write chronologically but included some other facts for us to ponder on. Likewise, after breaking the bread, the Lord took cup and when he had supped said, 'This cup is the new testament in my blood; this do ye, as oft as ye drink, in remembrance of me.

Each word said by Lord Jesus Christ at the time of Lord's Supper carries great significance. From Matthew 26:26 the noticeable phrases are: "As they were eating", "Jesus took bread", "and blessed it", "and brake it", "and gave it" , "to the disciples, "and said", "Take eat"; "this is my body"

77

"As they were eating" (Matt. 26:26) or "And as they did eat" (Mark 14:22) signifies that the Lord's Supper was instituted by Lord Jesus Christ, immediately after the Passover feast celebration.

The context where Jesus said, 'this is my body" in Gospels, appears at a place where there is description about Passover celebration. It was on the first day of the feast of unleavened bread; obviously it was on the night before his crucifixion. This has direct reference to the lamb that was killed one day before the 14th Nissan by the children of Israel in the land of Egypt in obedience to the commandment of LORD through Moses and Aaron to escape from the tenth plague that was brought by the LORD in Egypt.

The firstborn of every Egyptian, including that of Pharaoh, was killed on the night when the LORD Passed over the land. The LORD redeemed the children of Israel, who were in bondage of slavery under Pharaoh. Every firstborn of the children of Israel and their household was spared from the wrath of the LORD, because they did as He commanded them to do. They were asked to kill the lamb, set apart for this purpose, on the fourteenth day of the first month of the first year and strike its blood on the lintels and door posts of their houses. The LORD did as He said to them and passed over their homes on seeing the blood of the lamb on the lintels and door posts of their homes. The next morning they left the Egypt and enjoyed freedom.

The children of Israel were asked to keep Passover forever. Jesus, who came not to break the law, but to fulfill it, kept the Passover just before his crucifixion exactly as was required of him to do and in compliance to the instructions that were given in Exodus Chapter 12. It was the Passover feast day, and the disciples of Jesus asked him as to where would he have the feast of unleavened bread.

Luke's account of the Passover feast and Lord's Supper give few extra details such as a Jesus telling his disciples to follow a man bearing a pitcher of water, an unusual scene among Jews. The disciples are asked to follow him into the house where he enters. The disciples then were supposed to ask the man of the house that the Master wants to know where the guest chamber is, where He along with the disciples would eat the Passover meal. The man of the house shows a large upper room where Jesus would eat the Passover meal. The disciples did just as the Master, Lord Jesus told them to do.

When the hour came Jesus sat down with his twelve disciples and expressed how much he desired to eat the Passover meal with his disciples before he suffers. The disciples would have got perplexed to hear that Jesus was going to suffer. It was feast time. The unleavened bread was to be eaten in remembrance of God's mighty power that delivered the children of Israel from the bondage of Slavery in Egypt. It was a time for Jesus and his disciples to remember how the firstborn of every Egyptian was killed but every first born of the children of Israel was spared.

It was then that Jesus says that one of his twelve disciples, who were sitting with him, to dine with him, would betray him. It was a time to celebrate the happy moments of the children of Israelites, whose first born were spared, by the LORD, so that they may be delivered from the bondage of slavery under Pharaoh, and when the disciples heard about the betrayal of Jesus by one of them, they were utterly perplexed and disturbed. Each one of them questioned Jesus, if he was the betrayer of Jesus. Each one questioned him, "is it I?" Jesus said to them that he, who was dipping his hand with

80

Jesus, shall betray him. The one, who was dipping his hand with Jesus at that time, was Judas Iscariot.

Judas then asks Jesus if he was the one, who was going to betray him, and Jesus replied to him "Thou hast said". Before that Jesus said that the Son of man would go as it was written of him, but he who betrays him would be cursed and better if he were not born.

Judas Iscariot was also known "son of perdition", which means destined to destruction. Judas Iscariot was indeed destined to destruction. He did not have good life after betraying Jesus on the same night; rather "he cast down the pieces of silver in the temple, and departed, and went and hanged himself". (Matthew 27:5). Apostle Peter spoke of him saying "Now this man purchased a field with the reward of iniquity; and falling headlong, he burst asunder in the midst, and all his bowels gushed out" (Acts 1:18).

Jesus knew about the nefarious character of Judas Iscariot, and this is obvious when he said to Peter "…Have not I chosen you twelve, and one of you is a devil? He spake of Judas Iscariot the son of Simon: for he it was that should betray him, being

Leslie M. John

one of the twelve" (John 6:70-71) Simon Peter was curious to know as to who that disciple was, who was going to betray Jesus.

When Jesus was asked about it, he said he would hand over the sop to the disciple who was going to betray him and gave the sop to Judas Iscariot, the son of Simon. After the sop Satan entered Judas Iscariot, the son of Simon. Jesus said to Judas Iscariot to hasten doing what he had decided to do. None of his disciples, other than Judas Iscariot knew what would be the forthcoming events. Some of his disciples thought that Judas had a bag with him, and Jesus was asking to go ahead and buy some valuables for poor. Judas, having received the sop, left immediately. (John 13:24-30). This was the last time Judas was with Jesus as his disciple. It may be noted that Judas Iscariot participated in the Passover meal, but not in the Lord's Supper. The Lord's Supper followed the Passover meal.

From Luke's account we see that there were two cups, one of which was used during the Passover meal, and it was ceremonial cup. "And he took the cup, and gave thanks, and said, Take this, and divide it among yourselves" (Luke 22:17) Later, while instituting the Lord's Supper Jesus used another cup, which he called as, "…This cup is the new testament in my blood, which is shed for you".

"Likewise also the cup after supper, saying, This cup is the new testament in my blood, which is shed for you". (Luke 22:20)

Immediately after the Passover meal, "…Jesus took bread, and blessed it, and brake it, and gave it to the disciples, and said, Take, eat; this is my body. And he took the cup, and gave thanks, and gave it to them, saying, Drink ye all of it; For this is my blood of the new testament, which is shed for many for the remission of sins. But I say unto you, I will not drink henceforth of this fruit of the vine, until that day when I drink it new with you in my Father's kingdom. And when they had sung an hymn, they went out into the mount of Olives". (Matthew 26:17-30).

The Passover Lamb slain was a shadow of what was to come and fulfill in Jesus Christ. "Purge out therefore the old leaven, that ye may be a new lump, as ye are unleavened. For even Christ our Passover is sacrificed for us: Therefore let us keep the feast, not with old leaven, neither with the leaven of malice and wickedness; but with the unleavened bread of sincerity and truth" (1 Corinthians 5:7-8)

It is by Christ's sacrifice for our sins that our sins were passed over. Paschal lamb described in Exodus Chapter 12:5 was the type of Christ. We all are required to put away our sins before we can take part in his body and blood and be spiritually fed.

He was oppressed, and he was afflicted, yet he opened not his mouth: he is brought as a lamb to the slaughter, and as a sheep before her shearers is dumb, so he openeth not his mouth. (Isaiah 53:7)

"And I beheld, and, lo, in the midst of the throne and of the four beasts, and in the midst of the elders, stood a Lamb as it had been slain, having seven horns and seven eyes, which are the seven Spirits of God sent forth into all the earth". (Revelation 5:6)

We partake Lord's Supper to remember the death of Lord Jesus Christ, whom John pointed and said '...Behold the Lamb of God, which taketh away the sin of the world" (John 1:29). Jesus was crucified, buried, was raised on the third day, and ascended

Leslie M. John

into heaven. He is now seated on the right of the Majesty.

Is the Passover fulfilled once and for all with the institution of Lord's Supper? Passover was an everlasting commandment given to the children of Israel. Jesus said…" But I say unto you, I will not drink henceforth of this fruit of the vine, until that day when I drink it new with you in my Father's kingdom".

The scripture says that the Lord's Table will be removed from our midst when Jesus returns and our present way of remembering Lord's death, burial and resurrection by participating in the Lord's Supper will not be the same after we are "caught up". The Church is the body of Christ and the bride of Christ. Passover festival is not applicable to the Church.

Let us be glad and rejoice, and give honour to him: for the marriage of the Lamb is come, and his wife hath made herself ready. And to her was granted that she should be arrayed in fine linen, clean and white: for the fine linen is the righteousness of saints. And he saith unto me, Write, Blessed are they which are called unto the marriage supper of

Leslie M. John

the Lamb. And he saith unto me, These are the true sayings of God. (Revelation 19:7-9)

Immediately after the Passover meal, "...Jesus took bread, and blessed it, and brake it, and gave it to the disciples, and said, Take, eat; this is my body. And he took the cup, and gave thanks, and gave it to them, saying, Drink ye all of it; For this is my blood of the new testament, which is shed for many for the remission of sins. But I say unto you, I will not drink henceforth of this fruit of the vine, until that day when I drink it new with you in my Father's kingdom. And when they had sung an hymn, they went out into the mount of Olives". (Matthew 26:17-30)

Let us "do this in remembrance of me" until He comes as it is written...."For I have received of the Lord that which also I delivered unto you, That the Lord Jesus the same night in which he was betrayed took bread: And when he had given thanks, he brake it, and said, Take, eat: this is my body, which is broken for you: this do in remembrance of me. After the same manner also he took the cup, when he had supped, saying, This cup is the new testament in my blood: this do ye, as oft as ye drink it, in remembrance of me. For as

Leslie M. John

often as ye eat this bread, and drink this cup, ye do shew the Lord's death till he come. (1 Corinthians 11:23-26).

Yes! This Lord's Table is for us to remember Lord's death until he comes, and then there is no need of it because we will be with Him for ever and ever. We will see Him face to face. The Lord's Table will be removed from our midst. In a sermon named "The Feast of the Lord" Charles H. Spurgeon said... "The other mark of time in the text is "till he come." Then this service is to end. There will be no more Lord's Suppers when Christ appears, because they will be needless.

CHAPTER 13
THE REMEMBRANCE

"In the last day, that great day of the feast, Jesus stood and cried, saying, If any man thirst, let him come unto me, and drink. He that believeth on me, as the scripture hath said, out of his belly shall flow rivers of living water". (John 7:37-38)

Truly the Scripture has said it so in the Old Testament in Isaiah 58:11 (Cf. Isaiah 41:17-18, Isaiah 44:3-4, Joel 3:18)

"And the LORD shall guide thee continually, and satisfy thy soul in drought, and make fat thy bones: and thou shalt be like a watered garden, and like a spring of water, whose waters fail not".

It is about the outpouring of the Holy Spirit on those who are thirsty for Him. Without the Spirit of God man cannot be successful in anything. All things are possible with him and those who depend upon will be successful in their lives. Jesus said he will give his peace to us.

"Peace I leave with you, my peace I give unto you:

not as the world giveth, give I unto you. Let not
your heart be troubled, neither let it be afraid"
(John 14:27)

Jesus also promised before his crucifixion that he
will send the Promise of the Father (Luke 24:49). As
Jesus promised Holy Spirit came upon his disciples
who were waiting for Him. Later, as Jesus told
them they proclaimed the gospel of Jesus Christ,
first in Jerusalem, next in Judea and Samaria and
then to the uttermost part of the earth. All those
whose sins are forgiven are baptized in the Holy
Spirit and Holy Spirit indwells them from the
moment they are saved.

God's desire always has been that man may
remember his works, his love towards man. That is
why he became one like us and dwelt among us. He
will not tolerate any body worshipping idols. God
remembered Israelites who were willing to come to
him after hearing the warnings. God chastised the
children of Israel several times for worshipping
idols and committing sins, yet he was kind to them.
He called them "My people".

Jesus came into this world to save sinners.
Whoever believes in him will have everlasting life.

Leslie M. John

This is the promise of God.

"And the LORD spake unto Moses, saying, Speak unto the children of Israel, saying, The fifteenth day of this seventh month shall be the feast of tabernacles for seven days unto the LORD". (Leviticus 23:33-34)

The LORD asked the children of Israel to celebrate the 'feast of tabernacles' to remember the LORD's compassion, his protection and his provision to the children of Israel. The LORD said to them that they should dwell in booths during this period of the festival. This festival is celebrated that they and their children may recollect how God redeemed them from the bondage of slavery with his mighty hand and led them through the wilderness for forty years providing them food, clothing and shelter. Not only he provided them their needs but God came and dwelt among them.

The children of Israel were asked to offer an offering made by fire unto the LORD and they were not supposed to do any servile work therein. (Leviticus 23:33-42).Israelites celebrated this festival and they still celebrate. This festival will also be celebrated in the Kingdom of heaven during millennium by all those who enter the thousand-year-reign. As for New Testament believers a similar sacrament is given to remember Lord Jesus Christ's death, burial and resurrection and that is the "Lord's Supper". Jesus redeemed us from the bondage of sin. Jesus accepted worship and he also said He and the Father are one.

"And the multitudes that went before, and that followed, cried, saying, Hosanna to the Son of David: Blessed is he that cometh in the name of the Lord; Hosanna in the highest" Matthew 21:9

One of the best of ways of honoring is to remember him, his death, burial and resurrection besides working for him to the best of one's capability.

"For I have received of the Lord that which also I delivered unto you, That the Lord Jesus the same night in which he was betrayed took bread: And when he had given thanks, he brake it, and said, Take, eat: this is my body, which is broken for you: this do in remembrance of me. After the same manner also he took the cup, when he had supped, saying, This cup is the new testament in my blood: this do ye, as oft as ye drink it, in remembrance of me. For as often as ye eat this bread, and drink this cup, ye do shew the Lord's death till he come". 1 Corinthians 11:23-26

CHAPTER 14
SATAN THE OLD DRAGON

The first chapter of the first book in the Bible says God created everything and everything that He created was good. Doubtless, we then can say God did not create evil. God created Cherubim in perfection. Cherubim are plural of Cherub. Lucifer was one such Cherub who was created in perfection. Lucifer was in a very high standing among other cherubim, but from the address in Ezekiel 28:11-17

It is evident that God was addressing Lucifer in the King of Tyre. Lucifer exalted himself with pride to be equal with God and, therefore, God found iniquity in Lucifer, who became Satan, the adversary. Lucifer was full of wisdom, perfect in beauty and was adorned with precious metals such as sardius, topaz, diamond, the beryl, the onyx, the jasper, the sapphire, the emerald, carbuncle and gold. He was in Eden the garden of God, who set him upon the holy mountain of God.

Lucifer walked up and down in the midst of stones of fire. He was perfect when was created. This is

93

very clear that Lucifer is a created being. God created the beautiful Cherub, who became Satan by his own thoughts and actions. Lucifer sinned and exalted himself above God. There was iniquity found in Lucifer by God, who, therefore, said that He will surely cast Lucifer to the ground and he will be laid before kings that they may see him.

Lucifer said in his heart...

1. "I will ascend into heaven"

2. "I will exalt my throne above the stars of God"

3. "I will sit also upon the mount of congregation, in the sides of the north"

4. "I will ascend above the heights of the clouds" and

5. "I will be like the most High"

How art thou fallen from heaven, O Lucifer, son of the morning! how art thou cut down to the ground, which didst weaken the nations! For thou hast said in thine heart, I will ascend into heaven, I will exalt my throne above the stars of God: I will sit also upon the mount of the congregation, in the sides of the north: I will ascend above the heights of the

Leslie M. John

clouds; I will be like the most High. (Isaiah 14:12-14)

The wise man, King Solomon, said in Proverbs 16:18

"Pride goeth before destruction, and an haughty spirit before a fall"

Apostle Paul said in 2 Corinthians 11:14

"And no marvel; for Satan himself is transformed into an angel of light"

Satan, who went in the form of serpent, beguiled the woman, Eve, in the Garden of Eden

"And the LORD God said unto the woman, What is this that thou hast done? And the woman said, The serpent beguiled me, and I did eat". (Genesis 3:13)

The serpent was more subtle than any beast of the field and he said to the woman "Yea, hath God said, Ye shall not eat of every tree of the garden?" So cunning was the speech of this Old Dragon that the woman got cheated when he said that "Ye shall not surely die: For God doth know that in the day ye eat thereof, then your eyes shall be opened, and ye shall be as gods knowing good and evil". The woman ate the fruit of the tree and transgressed the commandment of God. She not only ate but gave it to man, who also ate and thus sin entered into this world.

When God spoke to the serpent in Genesis chapter 3, He was actually addressing the Satan in the serpent. Likewise when Jesus was asking speaking to Peter and saying, "get thee behind me, Satan", God was not saying that Peter was Satan, but He was addressing satanic thoughts in Peter.

When God spoke of a tyrant, He was addressing the Satan and Satanic forces behind the tyrant. In the verses cited above God was addressing the King of Tyre, a terror during his regime, just as Adolf Hitler in his time. There were also great tyrants on Old Testament period, like Og, the King Bashan, Goliath, and the Philistine.

The evil powers that exist today in the form of terror, adultery, fornication, pornography, murder, and other sins in the world are the result of satanic influences on human beings. The fight that we need to have should be directed to the Satan, more than the individual sins themselves.

If we fight against the disease by treating the

Leslie M. John

symptoms at the base level instead of controlling temporarily and superficially the sickness, then the disease could be healed fully. Similarly if we depend on God and lead a righteous life, a prayerful life, we will be able to control the sin that emanates from yielding to Satan. Satan is a hater of innocents, and children. This could be seen how Satan forced Pharaoh to kill children and Herod to kill children.

Therefore, he makes people to kill children through abortion. It is not sin if family planning is done, before the union of chromosomes with ovaries forming an ovum, but after the formation of the ovum, if it is destroyed, it is tantamount to killing the child.

Satan is the prince of this world. All power is given to him, so he was quite right in tempting Jesus Christ by assuring to give all that is in the world, if only Jesus worshipped him. But Jesus quoted scriptures and pointed to Satan, that it is written in scriptures to worship God and God alone. If we depend on Jesus Christ we can be triumphant over Satan and his powers in the light of the scriptures, which say that Satan cannot do anything to us, the children of God. Satan is a great deceiver, and a

97

cheat. Never worship Satan and Satanic powers. Satan will lead his followers to hell and finally into 'Lake of Fire".

"And the devil that deceived them was cast into the lake of fire and brimstone, where the beast and the false prophet are, and shall be tormented day and night for ever and ever". (Revelation 20:10)

"And death and hell were cast into the lake of fire. This is the second death". (Revelation 20:14)

Jesus Christ defeated Satan at the cross of Calvary. We have hope that Lord Jesus Christ will keep us from falling. Apostle Paul writes in Romans 16:20

"And the God of peace shall bruise Satan under your feet shortly. The grace of our Lord Jesus Christ be with you. Amen" (Romans 16:20)

CHAPTER 15
SATAN THE SYMPATHIZER

Satan is cunning, sympathizing, crafty, cheat, and a great deceiver. He comes to us in various forms; sometimes as an angel of light and sometimes as a roaring lion. He is the trickiest one anyone has ever seen in one's life. The garb he puts on while he approaches us differs from time to time. Consider the way he tempted Lord Jesus Christ when he was hungry after fasting for forty days and forty nights. It may be remembered here that Lord Jesus Christ was fully divine and fully human.

Apostle Paul described about Lord Jesus Christ as one "who being in the form of God thought it not robbery to be equal with God but made himself of no reputation and took upon him the form of a servant, and was made in the likeness of men" (Philippians 2:6-7)

The temper went to Lord Jesus Christ and said "If thou be the Son of God, command that these stones be made bread". Bur Jesus answered and said "It is written, Man shall not live by bread alone, but by every word that proceeds out of the mouth of God" (Matthew 4:2-4)

Consider the posture Satan takes when approaching frail and week in natural desires. Many portray Satan as a horrifying figure with protruding eyelids, thick eyelashes, and with horns, besides with black garments. Contrary to these portraits the Bible presents him as an angel of light. True, He comes to the follower of Lord Jesus Christ like an angel masquerading himself as an angel of light. 2 Corinthians 11:4 Isaiah chapter presents the true picture of Satan, who was once Lucifer, the chief angel in God's abode. He was once a morning star, son of dawn! But because of his rebel against God, he and his companions were brought down low and were cast in the depths of the pit.

"How art thou fallen from heaven, O Lucifer, son of the morning! how art thou cut down to the ground, which didst weaken the nations! For thou hast said in thine heart, I will ascend into heaven, I will exalt my throne above the stars of God: I will sit also upon the mount of the congregation, in the sides of the north: I will ascend above the heights of the clouds; I will be like the most High. Yet thou shalt be brought down to hell, to the sides of the pit". (Isaiah 14:12-15)

Leslie M. John

Satan went to Eve and talked in a very sweet way. Genesis 3:1 reads

"Now the serpent was more subtil than any beast of the field which the LORD God had made. And he said unto the woman, Yea, hath God said, Ye shall not eat of every tree of the garden?" (Genesis 3:1)

Eve got cheated at the sweet talk of Satan, and yielded to his persuasion. Consider the way Satan approached Lord Jesus Christ through Peter, who was the most loved disciple of his Master Jesus Christ. Satan entered him quietly and expressed his sympathy towards Jesus Christ, who was about to be crucified. The purpose of Jesus Christ coming in to this world was to bear our sins and die for our sins. The purpose was to shed his blood for our sake so that we may not be condemned for our sins. The purpose was to present us blameless to God the Father, who when sees us, sees us through the blood of His own Son and does not find any sin in us and appears our heart, soul and mind appear as crystal clear to us. Though our sins were like scarlet, they were made as white as snow says the LORD.

"Come now, and let us reason together, saith the

LORD: though your sins be as scarlet, they shall be as white as snow; though they be red like crimson, they shall be as wool" (Isaiah 1:18).

Satan did not want this purpose of Jesus Christ be defeated and expresses sympathy through Peter by saying, "...Be it far from thee, Lord: this shall not be unto thee" (Matthew 16:22).

But Lord Jesus turned to Peter and said, "...Get thee behind me, Satan: thou art an offence unto me: for thou savourest not the things that be of God, but those that be of men" (Matthew 16:23)

Lord Jesus Christ considered Peter as the stumbling block to him because he did not have in his mind the purposes of God but had purposes of men. Peter, once acknowledged Lord Jesus Christ as the Son of God, because it was revealed to him by the Father. Now in this situation, he mind was controlled by Satan, and, therefore, Lord Jesus addresses Satan in him that rebukes him.

Lastly but not least let us also know that Satan comes like a roaring lion looking for someone to devour. Peter in his first epistle says "Be sober, be vigilant; because your adversary the devil, as a roaring lion, walketh about, seeking whom he may

Leslie M. John

devour" (1 Peter 5:8).

The only way to overcome Satan is to depend on Lord Jesus Christ. We cannot defeat Satan with our own strength but can defeat him by the strength of Lord Jesus Christ in us. Satan is afraid of the very mention of the blood of Jesus Christ. Let us beware of Satan and his tricks.

"Put on the whole armour of God, that ye may be able to stand against the wiles of the devil". (Ephesians 6:11)

Even as the days and years passed by after God saved Noah from the deluge, his posterity forgot about the penalty their forefathers had to pay for sinning against God. So they continued in their sins; this time not just they violated what God intended them to be, but they decided to live in one place by constructing a huge tower around their city that they may not go out from there. This was against the will of God, who intended that they should spread forth and occupy the entire earth and subdue it. The generations that came from the loins of Noah thought they could build a huge tower so that they could comfortably live in one place.

Leslie M. John

God's purpose from the beginning was that man should be fruitful, multiply, replenish the earth, subdue it, have dominion over the fish of the sea, over the fowl of the air, and over every living thing that moves on the earth. (Genesis 1:28)

Even so, after the flood, Noah was commanded by God that his sons be fruitful, multiply and replenish the earth.

"And God blessed Noah and his sons, and said unto them, Be fruitful, and multiply, and replenish the earth". (Genesis 9:1)

As man tried to build Babel Tower, God thwarted his plans and destroyed the tower and confused the languages of mankind. God said that if people continued in unity their power will soon be exceedingly great which would be to the detriment of human beings. The LORD came down to see the city and the tower that they built and said that they have one language and if they continue to do this "nothing will be restrained from them, which they have imagined to do. Go to, let us go down, and there confound their language, that they may not understand one another's speech. So the LORD scattered them abroad from thence upon the face of all the earth: and they left off building the city. (Genesis 11:6-8). Notice, God said to Himself, "let us go down". There was plural used and from this phrase and other passages in the Scriptures it is evident that God is Triune.

The efforts on the part of man to construct a tower and live in one place and God spoiling their plans shows us man's imaginations and working against God are foolish. Lord Jesus said to Paul "It is hard for thee to kick against pricks".

"And he said, Who art thou, Lord? And the Lord said, I am Jesus whom thou persecutest: it is hard for thee to kick against the pricks" (Acts 9:5)

It is time atheists read the verse from Psalm 14:1 which says: "The fool hath said in his heart, There is no God. They are corrupt, they have done abominable works, there is none that doeth good". (Psalms 14:1)

CHAPTER 16
ATHEISM

Webster dictionary describes "Atheism" as Ungodliness, wickedness, a disbelief in the existence of deity, the doctrine that there is no deity". Basically, it is the unbelief in any religion that leads a person to practice atheism. They have one belief though; they believe there is no God.

Bible says:

"The fool hath said in his heart, There is no God. They are corrupt, they have done abominable works, there is none that doeth good. The LORD looked down from heaven upon the children of men, to see if there were any that did understand, and seek God. They are all gone aside, they are all together become filthy: there is none that doeth good, no, not one" (Psalms 14:1-3) it was a Psalm of King David to the chief Musician sing aloud.

The same verses of King David are given again to the chief Musician upon Mahalath, Maschil in Psalm 53:1-3

"The fool hath said in his heart, There is no God. Corrupt are they, and have done abominable iniquity: there is none that doeth good. God looked down from heaven upon the children of men, to see if there were any that did understand, that did seek God. Every one of them is gone back: they are altogether become filthy; there is none that doeth good, no, not one". (Psalms 53:1-3)

God said "Let there be light: and there was light.", "Let the waters under heaven be gathered together unto one place, and let the dry land appear; and it was so. And God called the dry land Earth." And "So God created man in his own image, in the image of God created he him; male and female created he them." And God blessed them, and God said unto them, be fruitful, and multiply and replenish the earth, and subdue it..." If that be the case why would He contradict His own creation and His own words? No He would not! If God did not give power to earth to have what we call "Center of gravity" we would not have been living on earth.

How do I not fall then if I climb a ladder and then try to prove God, whether or not He would sustain me? Is it not tantamount to ordering God to

Leslie M. John

contradict His own laws and in order to sustain me? If we were to be on Moon, Mars or some other planet and jump off a ladder we would not fall and injure ourselves, simply because there is "Center of Gravity" on this earth and it is not there on Moon, Mars, or any other planet. And, who has put all things in their places? It is God.

"Thou hast put all things in subjection under his feet. For in that he put all in subjection under him, he left nothing that is not put under him. But now we see not yet all things put under him". (Hebrews 2:8)

In fact God sustains His children when they are in danger. When Jesus calmed down the storm in the Sea He did not contradict His own laws but applied supernatural powers in Him over the laws of the nature in order to control the storm. If such a situation arises and it warrants Him to save His children He will not go back, rather He will certainly apply such greater laws that may be required in order to undermine the laws of the nature. But if we deliberately jump from the top of a ladder in order to prove God, it is tantamount to testing God and His power.

Leslie M. John

God will not yield to such testing and become our toy in the hands of man in order to prove Himself right. There was mob who cried at the time of Lord Jesus Christ's death upon the cross. They said, "He saved others; himself he cannot save. If he be the King of Israel, let him now come down from the cross, and we will believe him" (Matthew 27:42). Jesus did not come down from the cross to prove that He is the Son of God, but fulfilled the desire of the Father.

When Neil Armstrong was on the moon he was virtually flying. He was unable to walk on the moon. If life can persist there we would have all gone there, perhaps! The laws of nature came in to force with the creation of the world and were already there even before scientists have discovered them. Thy have just discovered the hidden truths and mysteries of God to certain extent. There is yet great deal for man to discover. Darwin's theory of evolution has proved to be wrong. It is ridiculous to think that man evolved from Ape.

There are mysteries and realities, which man could not fathom until now. Take a look at the structure of our own bodies and the intricate and complex functioning of the nervous system for example. Man could not find a cure for brain damage until now. Nervous system is so great that if all the nerves are straightened and stretched to form a straight line, they would run in to several miles. Now when I drive my car on an over bridge during early dawn hours of the day or in the nights I usually turn my head to right and to catch a glimpse of the beaming rays emitting out from the head lights of fast moving cars in different lanes.

My heart rejoices and my spirit soars so high that my soul praises my God for giving me such privilege to watch that scene. That is because I worked at a place where I thronged to catch glimpse of a light ray from an electric bulb; it was not anywhere near at least within a radius of eight to ten kilometers. But then if we look towards the sky in the night to watch the twinkling lights beaming out from the stars, and meditate on the ONE who created them, who would say that there is no God. How blessed are we that we can view these STARS and wonderful galaxy from any part of the world, not just from over bridge of an Interstate Highway. "The fool hath said in his heart, There is no God"

"Jesus saith unto him, I am the way, the truth, and

the life: no man cometh unto the Father, but by me". John 14:6

"For all have sinned, and come short of the glory of God;" Romans 3:23

"Jesus answered and said unto him, Verily, verily, I say unto thee, Except a man be born again, he cannot see the kingdom of God". John 3:3

Salvation is available freely for all who believe in Jesus Christ, confess his/her sins to Him, and accept Jesus Christ as his/her personal Savior and acknowledge Him as his/her Lord.

CHAPTER 17
SERVE THE LORD OR SATAN

(THERE IS NO MIDDLEWAY)

"And if it seem evil unto you to serve the LORD, choose you this day whom ye will serve; whether the gods which your fathers served that were on the other side of the flood, or the gods of the Amorites, in whose land ye dwell: but as for me and my house, we will serve the LORD". (Joshua 24:15)

"And the people said unto Joshua, Nay; but we will serve the LORD". (Joshua 24:21)

A similar but serious question was asked by Elijah and the people witnessed the fury and power of God. Then the fire of the LORD fell and burned up the sacrifice, the wood, the stones and the soil, and also licked up the water in the trench. 1 Kings 18:38. When all the people saw this, they fell prostrate and cried, "The LORD-he is God! The LORD-he is God!" 1 Kings 18:39. The same question lingers us around even today. Let those who have not chosen God even now, make a

Leslie M. John

decision today, lest God might show his anger towards the negligent and arrogant. God in his mercy sent in to this world, His one and only son, Jesus Christ, who died on the cross of Calvary on behalf of us, so that whoever believes in him shall not perish but have eternal life. Let us beware of Satan, and let us beware of his tricks.

Leslie M. John

CHAPTER 18
WHO DID SATAN ACT UPON

SIMON PETER OR JUDAS ISCARIOT

PETER

Simon Peter was a chosen vessel unto Jesus Christ and he spoke of Jesus as the Son of the living God. When Jesus asked his disciples as to what the people say about Him? Some said that they say He was John the Baptist, and others say Elias, or Jeremiah, or one of the prophets. Jesus, then, asked His disciples as to what they think of Him. Peter took advantage of that question and spoke boldly that He is the Son of the living God.

"And Simon Peter answered and said, Thou art the Christ, the Son of the living God" (Matthew 16:16)

Then, Jesus said to him that Peter was blessed because it was Father who revealed to him about Lord Jesus Christ, and that Peter was the part of the big rock, and on the rock he would build His Church. Jesus gave him great authority that the keys of the kingdom of heaven are given to him and whatever he binds on earth shall be bound in heaven, and whatever he loses on earth shall be loosened in heaven.

Jesus showed to His disciples as to how he should go to Jerusalem and suffer many things at the hands of elders, chief priests and scribes and be killed and raised again on the third day. Peter could not bear those words of Jesus and said to Him that such a thing should not happen to Him, but then Jesus said to him that he did not know the desires and plans of the Father. Peter boasted of himself that he would not deny Lord Jesus Christ but then Jesus said to him that he would deny Jesus three times before the cock crows.

And the Lord said, Simon, Simon, behold, Satan hath desired to have you, that he may sift you as wheat: But I have prayed for thee, that thy faith fail not: and when thou art converted, strengthen thy brethren. And he said unto him, Lord, I am ready to go with thee, both into prison, and to death. And he said, I tell thee, Peter, the cock shall not crow this day, before that thou shalt thrice deny that thou knowest me. (Luke 22:31-34)

On the night when Jesus was betrayed and was being taken for trail, Peter denied Jesus three times, and later cried bitterly (Matthew 26:75)

Leslie M. John

And the Lord turned, and looked upon Peter. And Peter remembered the word of the Lord, how he had said unto him, Before the cock crow, thou shalt deny me thrice. (Luke 22:61)

Peter was impulsive in nature and said that he would not deny Jesus Christ, but failed. He denied Jesus Christ three times before Jesus was crucified. Jesus looked back toward him as if to remind the falling nature of man. Peter went and cried for his failure. Notice Peter had called Jesus Christ as Lord even before he denied that he knew him.

Jesus rose from the dead on the third day and after His resurrection he was on this world for forty days. He appeared to many men and women before his ascension. Peter seemed unconcerned after the burial of Jesus Christ and said to his colleagues "I go fishing" and they followed him. As they were fishing they caught nothing. At this time Jesus appeared to them and stood on the shore, but His disciples did not recognize Him. Then, Jesus asked them, "Children, have ye any meat?" They answered, "No".

Jesus said to them to cast their nets on the right side of the ship assuring them a catch. They obeyed and cast their nets on the right side of the ship and they found much fish that it was hard for them to draw the net out. Simon Peter, who loved Jesus,

116

said "It is Lord". Immediately he recognized that Jesus spoke to him, he jumped into water because he was naked.

All the disciples came into ship and surprisingly they saw a fire of coals there and fish laid on it and bread. Jesus said to them to bring the fish that they caught. Simon Peter went up and drew the net, which was full with great fishes, a total of, one hundred and fifty three fishes, from waters to the land. Even though the net was full with great fishes, numbering one hundred and fifty three, the net did not break.

None of the disciples dared to ask Jesus who He was when He invited them to eat the food because they understood that He was Lord Jesus Christ. Jesus gave them bread and fish. This was the third time Jesus showed Himself to them after His resurrection.

After they ate food Jesus addressed Peter as "Simon Peter, son of Jonas" and asked him if he loved Lord Jesus Christ more than the other disciples. Although the word "love" is one in English, the usage in Greek was in three kinds.

The first one is "Eros" which means fleshly love, the love that is of worldly lusts. The second one is "Phileo" which is brotherly love and the thirdly love is the love that God shows towards mankind, which is 'agape' love.

When Jesus asked Peter whether or not he loved Jesus, He was referring to the love that exists between God and man; the agape love. But, Peter understood as brotherly love, "Phileo". Jesus said to Peter to feed His lambs. Jesus asked Peter second time if he loved Him and Peter again was referring to the love "Phileo" that he had towards Him. Jesus said to Peter to feed His sheep.

When Jesus asked Peter the third time expecting that peter would say that he had 'agape' love, Peter was grieved because Jesus asked him the third time whether or not he loved Jesus, and said to Him "Lord, thou knowest all things; thou knowest that I love thee". Jesus said to Peter to feed His sheep. Peter saw John come to them and he asked Jesus what John would do. Jesus replied what is it for him if He delayed coming and there was a misunderstanding among them that John would not die until Jesus comes again, but Jesus said "If I will that he tarry till I come, what is that to thee? follow thou me". That was John who wrote about the future coming of Lord Jesus Christ and his testimony is true (Cf. 21:3-5)

Leslie M. John

Peter's confession that Jesus is the Lord and the Son of the living God was much before his denial. His denial was equal to that of a backslider and coming back to Jesus Christ. His denial was not equal to refusing salvation.

His confession that Jesus is the Lord and the Son of the living God was much before his denial. His denial was equal to that of a backslider and coming back to Jesus Christ. His denial was not equal to refusing salvation.

JUDAS ISCARIOT

Judas Iscariot never worked for Lord Jesus; rather he worked against him. Judas Iscariot was called, 'son of perdition.' Though Judas was an ordinary man like any other disciple, yet he was the one who Satan used for his purposes.

Jesus knew who Judas was and what he would do to Him. Jesus, while praying to the Father in heaven, named Judas as, "son of perdition' and also asserted that he was lost. These things happened that Scriptures might be fulfilled. Judas yielded to Satan and in the love of money he yielded to Satan and Satan used him. (Cf. Luke 22:3, John 13:27)

Leslie M. John

CHAPTER 19
THIRTY PIECES OF SILVER

"Then was fulfilled that which was spoken by Jeremy the prophet, saying, And they took the thirty pieces of silver, the price of him that was valued, whom they of the children of Israel did value" (Matthew 27:9)

There is prophesy about the betrayal of Jesus Christ in Zachariah Chapter 11:12-13

"And I said unto them, If ye think good, give me my price; and if not, forbear. So they weighed for my price thirty pieces of silver. And the LORD said unto me, Cast it unto the potter: a goodly price that I was prised at of them. And I took the thirty pieces of silver, and cast them to the potter in the house of the LORD" (Zechariah 11:12-13)

God gave the children of Israel certain rules to follow as written in Exodus Chapter 21 in addition to the Ten Commandments that are recorded in Exodus Chapter 20. One such rule was the payment of compensation when an ox hurts. If an ox hurts a man or woman to such an extent that a man or

Leslie M. John

woman bleeds and the man or woman dies the ox shall be surely stoned and the flesh shall not be eaten. The owner of the ox shall be set free. But if the ox pushed any man or woman with its horn any time before and subsequently kills a man or woman not only the ox shall be stoned but the owner of the ox shall also be put to death.

There were also capital punishments detailed. But if the ox pushes a manservant or maidservant, the owner of the ox shall give to the master of the manservant thirty shekels of silver and the ox shall be stoned. (Exodus 21:28-32). The children of Israel valued thirty pieces of silver for a manservant or a maidservant (Exodus Chapter 21:32).

Apostle Paul wrote about Jesus that he was in the form of God but made himself of no reputation and came to this earth in the form of man and took the form a servant.

"Who, being in the form of God, thought it not robbery to be equal with God: But made himself of no reputation, and took upon him the form of a servant, and was made in the likeness of men" (Philippians 2:6-7)

Judas Iscariot demanded thirty pieces of silver as

121

compensation for betraying Jesus who came to this earth in the form of man. This was the price that was paid to Judas Iscariot for betraying Jesus. Our savior was made worth of thirty pieces of silver. That was the price of a manservant or a slave! However, the money that was paid as compensation to betray Jesus was made use of, for the salvation of Gentiles. The betrayal of Jesus was the fulfillment of prophecy mentioned in Zachariah 11:12-13.

Peter described Judas's betrayal of Jesus and his suicide in Acts Chapter 1:15-20. He said that the scripture was fulfilled. Judas fell headlong and he burst asunder and his bowels gushed out. Peter also had in his mind Psalms 69:26 and Psalms 109:8 when he was describing about Judas Iscariot.

Judas Iscariot betrayed Jesus and then realized that he did wrong to Jesus. Judas Iscariot brought the thirty pieces of silver to the chief priests and elders and said: "I have sinned in that I have betrayed innocent blood"; but they refused to accept the money back from Judas Iscariot. Judas cast down the thirty piece of silver in the temple and he left and hanged himself.

The chief priests took the silver pieces and put that money into the treasury because it was the price of blood. They took counsel and bought with that money the potter's field to bury in the strangers. The field is called as "The field of blood unto this day. (Matthew 27:3-10)

Jews thought the potter's field was the fittest place for burying strangers who came to Jerusalem and died. These strangers whom Jews considered as abominable were obviously Gentiles who came to attend feasts in Jerusalem. There was a provision made for the Gentiles in the land of Jews.

This potter's field is the place where strangers were buried. This field was purchased by the price of thirty pieces of silver as was prophesied. This potter's field is the burial place of Gentiles. Jesus paid his blood as the price for the salvation of entire mankind. Thirty pieces of silver was the price for buying the potter's field where strangers were buried. It is the field bought with the blood of the one who was crucified for us. He paid the price for the salvation of not only Jews but also the Gentiles.

CHAPTER 20
THE ACCUSER

Satan is also called as the Devil. It is "EVIL", just the opposite of "GOOD". Satan's work is to tempt us and push us into sinful life, to make us live life full of evil. When it comes to the usage of tongue, Satan, who is otherwise called Devil, makes us use it in an unworthy manner. Instead of using the tongue for praising God, and worshipping Him, Satan influences his followers to slander our brothers/sisters friends and enemies.

The word "Devil" is translated as "diabolist", which is also translated as slanderer that is one who makes false allegations against another. The book of Revelation depicts Satan as "the accuser (or slanderer) of the brethren". The followers of Satan like to accuse people by casting aspersions against them directly or sometimes indirectly.

Apostle Paul encouraged a young believer named Titus to request the members of his church not to accuse one another and warned them to be careful about what they talk. No doubt the caution was meant specifically to women in the church;

124

nevertheless everyone can take lessons from such exhortation. Paul knew that slander was of the devil and he also admonishes us to realize this fact.

May we realize that temptation comes from Devil (Satan, the accuser)? If we are the children of God and depend on Him, He will help us hold our tongue when we have devilish things to say. The tongue will no more be a devilish one then, but a praising and worshipping one. Let us consider one such case.

Leslie M. John

CHAPTER 21
SOVEREIGN GOD

OMNISCIENT, OMNIPRESENT AND OMNIPOTENT

"For there is not a word in my tongue, but, lo, O LORD, you know it altogether" Psalm 139:4

No one can cheat God, and from him nothing can be hid, for he is Omniscient, Omnipresent, and Omnipotent. King David realized that nothing can be hid before HIM because he is there everywhere, he knows everything about us. Every thought in us is known to him and He is all powerful. Hypocrisy lies and falsehood have no place before God. He knows everything and He is everywhere. The LORD is Omniscient, Omnipresent, and Omnipotent.

God's knowledge cannot be compared with any human being. His thoughts are higher than our thoughts, his ways are perfect and whatever he does it for our sake he does it with perfection and everything works for good for those who believe in him.

Man's greatest wisdom is foolishness before God,

Leslie M. John

yet man thinks he can reach God, he can emulate God, and he can become like God. It is only satanic belief that man can become like God. God is Omniscience, that is he has all the knowledge, he is present everywhere, and, therefore, he is Omnipresent and he has unlimited power and, therefore, he is Omnipotent.

God is so compassionate that he sent His one and only Son for our sake in to this world to bear our sins and redeem us from our sins and grant us eternal life. Wherever we go we find God because he is everywhere. The heaven is our God's throne and the earth is his footstool.

While proclaiming about himself, God says, he cannot be contained as an idol in men's temples, nor can he be worshipped there with animal sacrifices. All the saved Children of God, irrespective of their heredity whether they are from Jews or Gentiles, who believed that Jesus Christ is the Lord, will all be gathered to eternity. Isaiah 66:1 "Thus saith the LORD, The heaven is my throne, and the earth is my footstool: where is the house that ye build unto me? And where is the place of my rest?"

He is all powerful and watches over us. He has infinite power and authority on nature, because he is the creator and He created everything. His command is exceedingly authoritative, when he stands in the midst of great storm of wind that beat the ship, and calls for peace by rebuking the storm and wind. Mark 4:37 "And there arose a great storm of wind, and the waves beat into the ship, so that it was now full."

At the rebuke of Lord Jesus Christ storm calmed down and peace prevailed. Mark 4:39 "And he arose, and rebuked the wind, and said unto the sea, Peace, be still. And the wind ceased, and there was a great calm."

Should we not, therefore, acknowledge before we speak that God knows what our thoughts are, and what our intentions are? Let us humble ourselves and acknowledge the greatness of our God, and His leadership because He is wise, and is able to protect us from falling.

The writer of Hebrews says, Lord Jesus Christ is the express image of God, the Father in heaven.

"Who being the brightness of his glory, and the express image of his person, and upholding all

128

things by the word of his power, when he had by himself purged our sins, sat down on the right hand of the Majesty on high". Hebrews 1:3

Apostle Paul writes that Jesus Christ is the Creator and he is all powerful. Colossians 1:16-17 "For by him were all things created, that are in heaven, and that are in earth, visible and invisible, whether they be thrones, or dominions, or principalities, or powers: all things were created by him, and for him: And he is before all things, and by him all things consist." God became man for us and came down to this earth to save you and me. This is the day of salvation.

It is a great call to all creation to render their worship to the living God, who created heavens, earth, angels, animals, flying fowl, and creeping things by command. He took special care to create you and me. The glory of God is seen in his creation, everywhere under the sun, under the water, and upon the earth, and, therefore, it is the duty of every creature, who is in communication with God, that they praise him and worship him. The angels, whom God created to worship him and to minister and guard us, according to his command, should praise God.

Leslie M. John

The glory of God shines exuberantly in all his creation; therefore, every creation should praise him and worship him. Everything present in different spheres of heavens should praise God. Everything in heaven, one from the face of the earth to up to the clouds, second from clouds to the regions where constellation is present, and third above it, which is an infinite space, where Almighty Gods abides, should praise God. The heavens are his abode, and the earth is his footstool. The rain water in the region where clouds are present, should praise God. As we live in this sinful world, we seldom realize that there is far greater glory in the presence of God, where angels are praising him for ever and ever.

We are, therefore, required to praise the living one and only God, through his son, Jesus Christ, the creator and our redeemer, in the best possible manner, and to the best of our capacity. Great whales, monsters, fire, hail, stormy winds, mountains, hills, are not excluded from praising and worshipping God: they are also required to worship God. When it comes to trees, the psalmist desires that fruitful trees worship God. How sad it is that unfruitful trees do not get the privilege of worshipping him. (Cf. Psalm 148:1-14)

Leslie M. John

In John 15:4 Lord Jesus Christ said, "Abide in me, and I in you. As the branch cannot bear fruit of itself, except it abide in the vine; no more can ye, except ye abide in me".

Kings and princes of his world should praise God for the greater privileges and blessings they received from God. Young men and old men, children praise the Lord, for his name alone is worthy to be praised. The people of Israel, who are intimate to him and are chosen, should praise the name of the Lord, because they are endowed with blessings, and strength.

Leslie M. John

CHAPTER 22
ALL CREATION PRAISE THE LORD

Psalms 134:1-2 "Behold, bless you the LORD, all you servants of the LORD, who by night stand in the house of the LORD. Lift up your hands in the sanctuary, and bless the LORD."

Heaven and the entire host there in are created by God. Likewise earth and everything upon it and the seas and everything in it are created by God. No matter how many times we read Genesis Chapter 1, yet we long to read again and again. Every time we read Genesis Chapter 1 it is a new experience and there is a new revelation of thought in our minds. The creation is so great. When we to look at the sky and think about the Galaxy and the Milky Way, during nights we cannot help but praise God for the wonderful creation he made. We believers in Christ see God everywhere in His creation.

He is so wonderful. Let us think about our own creation. God created man in his own image. Let he sinned and lost the perfect image of God, yet when we think about the complex systems in our body, we wonder how great our God is. He created us for

132

worshipping God. The Creator's handiwork is clearly visible in us. It only needs to place simple faith in the Lord Jesus Christ to realize how great he is and how loving he is. Shall we praise, thank and bless the LORD for the wonderful creation.

Psalms 137:4 How shall we sing the LORD's song in a foreign land?

In this Psalm we read the desperate condition of the children of God, taken captive by the enemies. Their condition now in Babylon was pathetic and sympathetic. Added to that, the Babylonians are asking them to sing a song to their idols, in worship. Israelites, the children of God, are forced to sing song. In order to fulfill the desire of the Babylonians, these men of Zion, the children of God, sing song in the form of lamentation, not to please them, but asking questions as to how they could sing the song there in the land of enemies, when they are taken captive!

The Israelites now realize that were earlier protected by God, and were in safe hands, but they disobeyed and worshipped idols, thereby allowing themselves to be left alone without the help of God. The enemies could capture them and their

133

land. Israelites now repent, and remember their past happy life in the safe hands of God, and sing "If I forget you, O Jerusalem, let my right hand forget its cunning".

Psalms 137:5 The entire Psalm is about the repentance of their sins and their failures in their land, which caused them to fall in the hands of enemies. They also pray now, "Remember, O LORD, the children of Edom in the day of Jerusalem; who said, Raze it, raze it, even to the foundation thereof." Psalms 137:7 It clearly shows the spiritual condition of God's children, who were in the safe hands of God, but because they voluntarily worshipped idols, and sinned against the Almighty God, they fell in the hands of enemies, and now repent, for having forsaken God. They prayed in repentance.

Let the name of the Lord be glorified. I praise you my Lord my God for the salvation you gave to me.

CHAPTER 23
WORSHIP GOD IN SPIRIT AND IN TRUTH

Worship is the reverence paid to God. As believers in Lord Jesus Christ, we worship the Father through His Son, Lord Jesus Christ, according to the New Testament pattern, where Jesus takes the prominence in our worship.

Greek Strong's definition number for worship is: G4353 Transliterated word is " proskynçtçs" It means:

1) to kiss the hand to (towards) one, in token of reverence 2) among the Orientals, esp. the Persians, to fall upon the knees and touch the ground with the forehead as an expression of profound reverence 3) in the NT by kneeling or prostration to do homage (to one) or make obeisance, whether in order to express respect or to make supplication.

Jesus said:

"Therefore doth my Father love me, because I lay down my life, that I might take it again". John 10:17

135

"But the hour cometh, and now is, when the true worshippers shall worship the Father in spirit and in truth: for the Father seeketh such to worship him". John 4:23

"I and my Father are one" John 10:30

It is obvious here that the true worshippers will worship the Father in spirit and in truth and as the "Father" in heaven and Jesus are one the worship that we render to Jesus is acceptable to the Father in heaven. Here, it becomes necessary for us to know what exactly "worship" is. Worship according to New Testament pattern is not fleshly nor is it physical. God is Sprit, therefore, our worship should be in spirit and in truth and not physical nor should be fleshly (John 4:24).

We see in Old Testament the pattern of worship had in it, a physical structure called, Tabernacle, Priests with special clothing, Lamp stands, burning of incense, usage of musical instruments, and sacrifice of animals. These all give us physical and fleshly senses.

New Testament pattern of worship is based on Hebrews 9:11-12, where Jesus is seen as the high priest and perfect tabernacle, not made with the

Leslie M. John

hands of men, or with the blood of goats, or calves, but with his own blood, which he shed for us at the cross of Calvary, and obtained eternal redemption for us.

We are no more strangers and foreigners but fellow citizens with the saints. Jesus Christ is the corner stone and in him we are built together for a habitation of God through the Spirit. (Ref. Ephesians 2:19-22)

New Testament pattern of worship is centered on Jesus Christ, and spiritual aspects of life. The believers in Christ are one household of God and are built on the foundation laid by the Apostles and Prophets. Lord Jesus Christ himself is the corner stone of such building. All those saved in the precious blood of Jesus are fitly framed together and grow in the grace of God and are parts of that holy temple of the Lord. We are built together for habitation of God through the Sprit.

Every born again child of God may worship God in spirit and in truth. Let us bow down to him and acknowledge him as our Lord and Savior. Let us sing songs and hymns of worship. Such worship rendered by the child of God is acceptable unto him.

Participation in Lord's Supper is not the only way of worshipping God, but it is one of the ways. Lord's Supper is to remember the death of our Jesus Christ. "For as often as ye eat this bread, and drink this cup, ye do shew the Lord's death till he come". Corinthians 11:26

Many times while remembering the death of Lord Jesus Christ the fact about his resurrection and ascension is undermined or forgotten. There is no reason to undermine to acknowledge the resurrection and his ascension while remembering about Lord Jesus Christ's death. We should not undermine to remember the resurrection of Lord Jesus Christ.

The observance of "Lord's Supper" by breaking bread and drinking from the cup is a great way of worshiping Lord Jesus Christ. We remember the death of Jesus Christ, his burial and resurrection and his ascension.

"And when he had given thanks, he brake it, and said, Take, eat: this is my body, which is broken for you: this do in remembrance of me. After the same manner also he took the cup, when he had supped, saying, This cup is the new testament in my blood: this do ye, as oft as ye drink it, in remembrance of me". (1 Corinthians 11:24-25)

Leslie M. John

CHAPTER 24
RELATIONSHIP OF JESUS WITH FOLLOWERS

John Chapter 10 deals with the subject of the relationship between him and those who have accepted him as the Lord. The comparison of the shepherd and his flock with Jesus his beloved ones is that Jesus is good shepherd. He is the door and there is no other way to the pasture. A thief does not enter the sheepfold by the door, but enters climbing the wall and entering some other way. Jesus said, if any man enters by Him he shall be saved.

A good shepherd gives life for his flock, but a hireling does not give his life. Hireling would run away leaving sheep helpless, when he encounters some danger. On the contrary, a good shepherd will leave ninety nine sheep aside and seek after the lost one sheep, and finds it and brings it back to the flock. Jesus is our good shepherd. 'I am the good shepherd, and know my sheep, and am known of mine '.

The word, 'know ' here shows the love that the sheep show toward their good shepherd, whom they trust and obey. Jesus asserts here that he is the good shepherd, who will not let his sheep be stolen by his enemy. He would leave ninety nine sheep aside for some time to go in search of one lost or backslidden sheep to bring it back to join the ninety nine.

John 10:27-30 'My sheep hear my voice, and I know them, and they follow me: And I give unto them eternal life; and they shall never perish, neither shall any man pluck them out of my hand. My Father, which gave them me, is greater than all; and no man is able to pluck them out of my Father's hand. I and my Father are one. John 10:14 'I am the good shepherd, and know my sheep, and am known of mine '.

Jesus Christ is the Son of God and very God Himself. Jesus said, in John 10:30 'I and my Father are one '. He said in John 16:15 'All things that the Father hath are mine: therefore said I, that he shall take of mine, and shall shew it unto you '. He said in John 17:11 'And now I am no more in the world, but these are in the world, and I come to thee.

Holy Father, keep through thine own name those whom thou hast given me, that they may be one, as we are '. Apostle Paul wrote about Jesus Christ in Colossians 1:15-18 'Who is the image of the invisible God, the firstborn of every creature: For by him were all things created, that are in heaven, and that are in earth, visible and invisible, whether they be thrones, or dominions, or principalities, or powers: all things were created by him, and for him: And he is before all things, and by him all things consist. And he is the head of the body, the church: who is the beginning, the firstborn from the dead; that in all things he might have the preeminence.

When we think of the sin King David did by committing adultery with Bathsheba we cannot think of any reason why God would not forgive our sins.

David was blessed one, God chose him to be King, yet one day when [2Sam 11th Chapter] saw from the roof of his home, a beautiful woman named Bathsheba washing herself. David sent messengers and took her, and committed sin with her. He did not end his iniquity there but conspired and got her husband, Uriah, killed in the battle. God punished

David for his sin. David's son from Bathsheba died, and David had to pay great penalty for his sin. Yet, when David repented of his sin, He had compassion on him and forgave him, and restored him.

Jesus became poor for us even though he was rich in his glory and was with the Father from eternity. He said he is the beginning and he is the end; he is the Alpha and Omega. He is the creator of this universe, he owns everything, every creation and he is the King of kings, he is the Lord or lords, and he is the God of gods.

CHAPTER 25
THE MINISTRY: PETER AND PAUL

"But when I saw that they walked not uprightly according to the truth of the gospel, I said unto Peter before them all, If thou, being a Jew, livest after the manner of Gentiles, and not as do the Jews, why compellest thou the Gentiles to live as do the Jews?" (Galatians 2:14)

PAUL REBUKES PETER

Apostle Paul rebuked Apostle Peter on a reason and that was surely a very stiff and open rebuke. It was not a private rebuke or admonition but a strong reproof of what Peter did. Did Peter deserve rebuke? According to the prevailing situation the rebuke was appropriate. Man is saved by grace through faith in Jesus and not by works or Mosaic Law. Paul surely taught the right doctrine about salvation. But did Peter and Paul preach different gospels? No. If Peter preached different Gospel he could be called accursed.

"But though we, or an angel from heaven, preach

any other gospel unto you than that which we have preached unto you, let him be accursed" (Galatians 1:8).

Did you hear anyone giving more importance to Paul than to Peter? Beware of doctrines from such an one! Either he is misguiding out of innocence or deliberately diverting to another doctrine! All the disciples preached salvation by Grace through faith in Jesus. Peter's audience was initially of Jews and he was obedient to the commission from Jesus. Peter and Paul had different assignments in the beginning, but not to cover their whole ministry. Peter was hypocritical when he sat to eat with Gentiles and then he withdrew from them on seeing when he saw James and others.

"For before that certain came from James, he did eat with the Gentiles: but when they were come, he withdrew and separated himself, fearing them which were of the circumcision". (Galatians 2:12)

That was the reason why Paul said …

"But when Peter was come to Antioch, I withstood him to the face, because he was to be blamed". (Galatians 2:11)

Leslie M. John

Paul spoke on Peter's face so confidently and bluntly that Peter was wrong on his hypocritical behavior thus affirming that Paul was equal in status as of Peter and other disciples to be called as an Apostle of Jesus Christ. Paul's confrontation with Peter was like an younger brother pointing a mistake of elder brother openly because of the offense elder brother had caused openly. Paul said that the Gospel of preaching to Jews was given to Peter and of Preaching to Gentiles was given to Paul.

(For he that wrought effectually in Peter to the apostleship of the circumcision, the same was mighty in me toward the Gentiles:) (Galatians 2:8)

We do not have sufficient evidence in the Scriptures about the time gap between Peter's preaching to Jewish audience and to Cornelius, an uncircumcised Gentle and then to other Gentiles. It is purely speculation that Peter did not preach to Gentiles. Peter surely knew the commission given in Acts 1:8. Peter did not retort at the rebuke of Paul; but rather he supported Paul at Jerusalem council in very gentlemanly way.

"And when there had been much disputing, Peter

Leslie M. John

rose up, and said unto them, Men and brethren, ye know how that a good while ago God made choice among us, that the Gentiles by my mouth should hear the word of the gospel, and believe". (Acts 15:7)

Peter approved Paul's message, which shows that Paul is not greater than Peter to say that God gave Paul an extra-ordinary authority over Peter and on doctrines. This a very strong point a group of believers contend saying Paul had the authority over the doctrines of salvation to Gentiles.

"And account that the longsuffering of our Lord is salvation; even as our beloved brother Paul also according to the wisdom given unto him hath written unto you " (2 Peter 3:15)

Before we go further on why Paul rebuked Peter it would be better to know What Jesus said about Peter. The word 'Church' appears in the New Testament first in Matthew 16:18 where Jesus said to Peter that He was the rock upon which Jesus would build His Church and that the gates of hell shall not prevail against it.

The Lord added to the Church daily such as should be saved (Acts 2:47). But if we closely ponder on

147

the personal behavior and Character of Peter we see that Peter was always very quick to take some decision and then repent; he was rather impetuous, or impulsive. Peter said he would not deny Jesus but denied Jesus and later repented. When Jesus spoke of his forthcoming death, Peter said it should not happen and Jesus said to Peter "Get thee behind me, Satan" Matthew 16:22, 23).

When Jesus was about to wash Peter's feet he resisted and Jesus said to Peter that if He did not wash Peter's feet he would not have part with Jesus. Then, Peter said to Jesus "... Lord, not my feet only, but also my hands and my head. (John 13:9). After resurrection of Jesus Peter said "I go fishing" rather than showing interest in finding where Jesus was (John 21:3) and just after a while when Peter saw Jesus his reaction is seen in John 21:7

"Therefore that disciple whom Jesus loved saith unto Peter, It is the Lord. Now when Simon Peter heard that it was the Lord, he girt his fisher's coat unto him, (for he was naked,) and did cast himself into the sea"

But then it was Apostle Peter who proclaimed the

Leslie M. John

Gospel of Salvation first. The first ever preaching of Jesus Christ's death, burial and resurrection was done by Apostle Peter, who was the beloved disciple of Lord Jesus Christ. Peter stood up in the midst of the disciples, and gave few details (Acts 1:15) and then in Acts 2:24 declared that God raised Jesus from the death.

"Whom God hath raised up, having loosed the pains of death: because it was not possible that he should be holden of it" (Acts 2:24)

When Saul was encountered by Lord Jesus Christ as narrated in Acts 9 Peter was already getting ready to preach to Cornelius, an un-circumcised Gentile.

And it came to pass, that he tarried many days in Joppa with one Simon a tanner. (Acts 9:43).

Thereafter, we read in Acts 10 Peter's preaching to Cornelius and about conversion of Cornelius. Paul was chosen to bear the name of Jesus before 'GENTILES', and 'KINGS', and the Children of Israel.

"But the Lord said unto him, Go thy way: for he is a chosen vessel unto me, to bear my name before the Gentiles, and kings, and the children of Israel"

Leslie M. John

(Acts 9:15)

Lord Jesus gave to his disciples commission that was applicable to Apostle Paul as well and that was to preach first to the Jews and then to Gentiles. Paul obeyed this commission and preached first to Jews and then to Gentiles.

"But ye shall receive power, after that the Holy Ghost is come upon you: and ye shall be witnesses unto me both in Jerusalem, and in all Judaea, and in Samaria, and unto the uttermost part of the earth". (Acts 1:8)

Paul was a Jew and a Pharisee and, therefore, he had much concern for his own people just as Jesus, who is born in Jewish family, had much concern for his own people first and then to the Gentiles. Paul says in Philippians 3:4-8 that he was circumcised on the eighth day, of the stock of Israel, of the tribe of Benjamin, a Hebrew of the Hebrews. He had much zeal for keeping Mosaic Law and, therefore, persecuted the church before his conversion.

After conversion he counted every gain in this world as loss for the sake of Christ. He acknowledged that Jesus was his Lord and considered every gain that had as 'dung' that he may win Christ. Paul also said in Romans 11:1 that he was an Israelite, of the seed of Abraham, of the tribe of Benjamin.

Paul's Roman citizenship by birth was an added qualification for him because many bought Roman Citizenship with a price paid for it but he was by birth a Roman Citizen. He was born in city of Tarsus, the capitol of Cilicia in Asia Minor (Ref. Nave's Topics), a city of southern Turkey, which was ruled by Roman Government (Acts 9:11, Acts 16:37, Acts 22:25-28)

"I say then, Hath God cast away his people? God forbid. For I also am an Israelite, of the seed of Abraham, of the tribe of Benjamin". (Romans 11:1)

The purpose of his laying emphasis on the fact that he was an Israelite, of the seed of Abraham, of the tribe of Benjamin was to say that in spite of his elite position in the Jewish lineage he had chosen to give out Gospel message to Gentiles. The doctrines that he preached were never preached earlier. Even Peter's early preaching differed from what Paul taught.

Paul was inspired by Jesus Christ to preach the Gospel of Grace to the world. This preaching was in

151

contradiction to the preaching of Judaism, and, therefore, he had to suffer much persecution. Once he was following Judaism, but then he turned against Judaism and preached Gospel of Grace. Paul preached that man is not saved by Law and works but by Grace alone. Paul said in Romans 1:16 that he was not ashamed of the Gospel of Christ because it is the power of God unto salvation to all those who believe, first to Jews and then to Gentiles. (Romans 1:16)

Apostle Paul's preaching which differed from what Judaism preached resulted in commotion, rebellion and refutations from among Jews. This was the first time Jews were listening to what Paul was saying that circumcision was not necessary to be saved; man is saved by Grace by faith in Jesus and not by works etc. Jews then rose and persecuted him.

Peter preached to Jewish audience who believed in signs that repentance was necessary for salvation followed by baptism, although he did not insist that baptism is mandatory for salvation.

"Then Peter said unto them, Repent, and be baptized every one of you in the name of Jesus Christ for the remission of sins, and ye shall receive

Leslie M. John

the gift of the Holy Ghost". (Acts 2:38)

On the contrary Apostle Paul did not preach that Baptism is necessary for salvation. His main emphasis was on believing on Lord Jesus Christ and confessing with your mouth that God raised Jesus Christ from the dead. Then, there is a question. Was Paul baptized and did he baptize? Acts 9:18 says that he was baptized.

1 Corinthians 1:13-17 show that Paul baptized and yet he says he was sent to preach the Gospel and not to baptize. Was he contradicting himself? No, what he meant was that while preaching the Gospel was his main focus baptism was secondary; that is to say baptism was not necessary for salvation. Baptism is an external evidence of internal repentance and accepting Jesus as personal savior, who died for our sin, buried and was rose from the dead on the third day.

"That if thou shalt confess with thy mouth the Lord Jesus, and shalt believe in thine heart that God hath raised him from the dead, thou shalt be saved. For with the heart man believeth unto righteousness; and with the mouth confession is made unto salvation." (Romans 10:9-10)

Leslie M. John

Paul also preached that no man should judge another in respect of eating meat or in drink or in respect of holidays, or the new moon, or of the Sabbath days.

"Let no man therefore judge you in meat, or in drink, or in respect of an holyday, or of the new moon, or of the sabbath days" (Colossians 2:16)

Unfortunately, some Christians show Paul superior to Peter and cause divisions among Christians. Notice IF the Church did not start until transition period of early Christianity was completed at Acts Chapter 28, THEN Paul was not in the "Body of Christ" for nearly thirty years. That was not true.

Peter and Paul had different duties to perform as per the commission. Peter, Paul and we are all one Body through Lord Jesus Christ (Galatians 3:14, Romans 12:4, 5). The "Body of Christ" which is the "Church" did not start in Apostle Paul but it started in Lord Jesus Christ.

And he is the head of the body, the church: who is the beginning, the firstborn from the dead; that in all things he might have the preeminence. (Colossians 1:18)

Leslie M. John

CHPATER 26
PRIVILEGES OF GENTILES

Peter, one of the disciples of Jesus Christ, says we are all sojourners on this earth. Our true inheritance, which is incorruptible, and that does not fade away, is in heaven. As aliens on this earth we enjoy all the privileges of citizens, yet our true treasure, that does not perish, is in heaven. Therefore, we should greatly rejoice. The price paid for us to have this great inheritance is the blood of Jesus Christ on the cross of Calvary. No amount of good works can save a person, and the only way to receive salvation is by the grace of God, through faith in him.

There are only three occasions shown in the Old Testament, when the blood was sprinkled. First one was when a covenant was established (Exodus 24:5-8), the second one was when Aaron and his sons were anointed as priests (Exodus 29:21), and the third one was when an unclean leper was cleansed (Leviticus 14:6-7). Now, when we apply this to ourselves, New Testament believers, it is so true that a covenant was established with the sprinkling of the blood of Jesus Christ, we are all made priests unto him, and we, who were unclean,

Leslie M. John

are cleansed from our sin. We are saved and made a new creation (2 Corinthians 5:17).

 The sacrifice of Jesus Christ bearing our sin upon the cross enabled us to approach the Father in heaven, through His only begotten son, Jesus Christ, who is our mediator. The blood of Jesus cleansed us from our sin. Although our temptations are manifold, yet the trial of our faith is much more precious than that of gold, which perishes. (1 Peter 1st Chapter)

If we call on the Father, He will help us that we pass our pilgrimage on this earth in fear of Him, rendering to Him His due worship. We are not redeemed by silver or gold, but by the blood of His only begotten Son Jesus Christ, whom John identified as the Lamb of God. Peter confirms that this Lamb of God was Lord Jesus. John said this is the Lamb of God came to this world to take away the sin of the world.

 The Father in heaven judges every man according to his/her works while sojourning on this earth. He keeps record of our vain conversations that we may have received from our earthly fathers following traditions.

Leslie M. John

Therefore, let us keep in mind that as the Scripture says, Lord Jesus Christ was 'foreordained before the foundation of the world' and he was revealed unto us in the form of man. He died on the cross, bearing our sins, so that we may have redemption from sin. God raised him from the dead on the third day after crucifixion. Jesus is not dead lying in the grave just as any other man; but he was raised from the dead on the third day as prophesied. Later, after forty days on this earth he ascended into heaven. He is now seated on the right hand of the Majesty, pleading on our behalf with the Father. Our faith in God increases as our days pass on this earth because of this infallible truth.

Our souls are purified by believing on this truth and hope increases as our sojourning on this earth tapers to start afresh eternal life with the only one, who paid the price for our salvation. Likewise, our love for one another should be fervent and pure. Just as grass withers, and flower fades, our life on this earth is also temporal and temporary, but the life with Jesus is eternal as the Word of God endures for ever. (I Peter 1st Chapter)

Peter goes on to reveal another great truth that we love our Lord, not because of we are able to see

Leslie M. John

him physically, but because of our belief in him. 1 John 4:19 we read that 'We love him, because he first loved us'.

Our savior, as described in Song of Solomon 5th Chapter, is 'altogether lovely' and ' white and ruddy, the chiefest among ten thousand'. Yet, it is not the beauty or the physical appearance of our Lord that makes us to love him but because he has shown his love toward us by shedding his precious blood for our sake in order that we may not be condemned but be saved. This was the way for our redemption from our sin. He is the way, the truth and the life. There is no one, except Jesus, who can save us from the eternal damnation. That is the reason why after having been saved we \'rejoice with joy unspeakable and full of glory\'.

We have received salvation of our souls by faith in him and the efficacy of his blood shed for us, rather than any works associated with law. Our salvation is not by any good works that we do or have done, but it is by believing in him through faith.

The Old Testament prophets have enquired about this salvation. They prophesied about the grace and about the salvation that will be available

Leslie M. John

through the only begotten Son of God. They prophesied about the sufferings of Jesus and the glory that he would have thereafter. Although they prophesied about these things, yet these were reserved for us to hear about and believe.

The angels desired to look into these things, but it was for us to have that privilege to hear and believe. The gospel of Jesus Christ is preached unto us, and it is great privilege for those who hear the good news about Jesus Christ to accept his sacrifice on the cross for our sake.

Peter, therefore, asks us to gird up the loins of our minds, be sober and hope for the grace that is to be brought unto us at the revelation of Jesus Christ. He asks us to follow Jesus who was holy and be as obedient children. We should neither lust nor live in fashion with an idea of attracting the other gender into lustful thoughts. Our conversation should bring glory and honor unto our Lord Jesus. (1 Peter 1:8-17)

CHAPTER 27
GRACE ABOUNDS

SIN SHALL NOT HAVE DOMINION

Peter and John, the disciples of Jesus Christ, preached the Gospel and the resurrection from the dead. They healed an impotent man in the name of Jesus. Their ministry was blessed and the number of believers increased from three thousand to five thousand. This kind of preaching, and miracles, in the name of Jesus, grieved the high priest Annas, Caiaphas, John, and Alexander, who thought that the preaching belonged to them, and there is no resurrection from the dead.

The Pharisees and Sadducees did not believe in the resurrection, and as they were against this teaching they laid hands on Peter and John, the disciples of Jesus, for a trial the next day. The elders, scribes, Annas, the high priest and high priest's kindred gathered at Jerusalem and questioned the authority by which they healed the impotent man, and preached the resurrection from the dead.

Peter, then, filled with Holy Spirit, spoke to them

Leslie M. John

and said to them very firmly that they preached and healed the impotent man in the name of Jesus Christ of Nazareth, whom they crucified, and whom God raised from the dead.

Jesus is the stone, who these elders, Pharisees, Sadducees rejected, but God set him as the Chief corner stone. David prophesied about Jesus, who was the stone, that the builders rejected, yet the LORD made him the head stone of the corner.

Peter and John, the disciples of Jesus, who walked with him, witnessed that Jesus was the stone, whom the Jews rejected, but he became the head stone of the corner. They affirm that there is no other name under heaven where anyone can find salvation.

One may object to this preaching but the Bible says it very firmly that there is no salvation except by believing that Jesus is the Savior. Peter and John, the Apostles, who were not learned, or educated, boldly said these things because they were with Jesus and took knowledge from him, who is the only begotten Son of God. The accusers attempted to execute the disciples of Jesus but did not find any cause to punish them, and let them go.

Leslie M. John

(References Acts 4:1-14, Ps 118:21-23. Isa. 28:16, Ro 9:33, Ephesians 2:20, 1Pe 2:7)

"And God is able to make all grace abound toward you; that ye, always having all sufficiency in all things, may abound to every good work" (2 Corinthians 9:8)

Sin shall not have dominion over born-again child because he is not under the law, but under grace. By one man's disobedience many were made sinners and so by the obedience of one shall be many made righteous. The righteousness does not confine to only many as few understand, but to all those who confess their sins to God and accept Jesus as their personal Savior. The law pointed the guilt of a person but the salvation is through the grace by faith in Jesus Christ. In him alone is salvation and there is no other way for being with him for ever and ever.

Where sin abounded grace did much more abound and that is the reason why no matter how serious is the sin a man may have committed, except for blasphemy of the Holy Spirit, there is forgiveness in Jesus. Sin brought death but grace from Jesus gives us eternal life. Jesus Christ is our Lord and he is

Leslie M. John

faithful to forgive us our sins.

What shall we say then, should we continue in sin that grace may abound. Apostle Paul says "God forbid". We who are dead to sin will not live in sin any longer. We are baptized into Jesus Christ into his death. (Romans 5:19-21 and Romans 6:1-3)

Those who seek to do good works and earn salvation by their own works do nullify the importance of blood of Jesus Christ. The blood of Jesus Christ that cleanses the sin has no value for them. They diligently keep doing good works in order to receive salvation neglecting the repeated emphasis from the Lord Jesus Christ that there is eternal life only in and through him. As we read in 2 Corinthians 9:8 God is able to make grace abound to every good work. But good works are not the way for salvation. The good works follow when a man is born-again.

The blood of Jesus shed on the cross of Calvary can only save a person. This is the only way to receive eternal life. Salvation is available to all those who go to him and accept him as the Lord.

Now, here is the question :

After having been delivered from the bondage of sin by grace through faith should a child of God keep sinning because he is under the grace but not under law?

No. Never should a child of God return to sin and lose blessings from God. Salvation is not lost for those who are saved in the blood of Jesus Christ; however, the Scripture does not endorse repeated sinning. God will surely chide and chastise the one that falls repeatedly into sin and seeks grace time and again.

Should we not consider the fact that if we yield to sin we are servants to sin; and sin becomes our master? We are under grace and we should remain servants to our Lord and be obedient to put on Christ as written in Ephesians 4:24.

We were, once servants of sin; but after accepting Jesus as our master, we have become servants of righteousness. We should bear fruit unto the Lord by leading a life of holiness and have assurance that there is everlasting life for us in eternity. The law has concluded all of us under sin, but the gift of God is eternal life through Lord Jesus Christ.

"And that ye put on the new man, which after God

is created in righteousness and true holiness".
(Ephesians 4:24)

****

Leslie M. John

Leslie M. John